SMOKY, THE UGLIEST CAT IN THE WORLD

and Other Great Cat Stories

Compiled and edited by
Joe L. Wheeler

Pacific Press® Publishing Association
Nampa, Idaho
Oshawa, Ontario, Canada
www.pacificpress.com

Cover art by Lars Justinen

Designed by Justinen Creative Group

Interior illustrations from the library of Joe L. Wheeler

Copyright © 2005
Pacific Press® Publishing Association
Printed in the United States of America

Additional copies of this book are available by calling toll free 1-800-765-6955 or by visiting www.adventistbookcenter.com

Library of Congress Cataloging-in-Publication Data

Smoky, the ugliest cat in the world : and other great cat stories/compiled and edited by Joe L. Wheeler.
p. cm. — (The good Lord made them all)
ISBN 13: 978-0-8163-2121-6
ISBN 10: 0-8163-2121-3
1. Cats—United States—Anecdotes. I. Wheeler, Joe L., 1936– II. Series.

SF445.5.S645 2005
636.8—dc22   2005051448

www.joewheelerbooks.com

08 09 10 11 · 5 4 3 2

DEDICATION
to
Pandora

Pandora, a beautiful Himalayan cat, ruled our book-laden house for thirteen and a half years. Born in Michigan, she lived with us for nine years in our home on Maryland's Severn River and in our Colorado mountain chalet for over four more.

Pandora was extremely selective in terms of to whom she opened up her heart. Only for us in the family—and even here she had her favorites—did her love come into full flower.

If I was trying to get a project done, in short order, I could count on her assumption that all priorities must start with her. She'd jump up on my desk or lapboard and demand my full attention.

At night, just as soon as we crawled into bed, regular as clockwork (usually within ninety seconds), we'd first feel a soft landing at our feet, and then we'd hear Pandora purring her way toward the pillows, where she'd butt our hands until her bewhiskered head received the required number of strokes. She'd stay with us all night.

We hated to leave her, for whenever we'd return from trips, she'd broken-heartedly sob her way through the house night after night, certain she'd been abandoned again (after all, three weeks in a cat's life seems like an eternity).

Finally, her internal organs ceased to function very well. To save her from further pain, we drove her to the vet. There, I took her into my arms and told her how very much we loved her. After the injection, her head just got heavier and heavier as her life ebbed away.

Afterward, I went out into the parking lot and wept.

Thus it is fitting that I dedicate this book of cat stories to our beloved cat, who still lives in our hearts—

Pandora

CONTENTS

INTRODUCTION

The Cat Dimension of Our Lives

-*Joseph Leininger Wheeler*-

Half of civilization is partial to cats, and half to dogs. Of all the animals and birds that God put on this planet, only these two species have women, men, and children really taken to their hearts; taken them into their homes; taken them into their daily lives.

How long cats have shared their lives with humans is anyone's guess. Documented history, however, traces them all the way back to Egypt, over 3,500 years ago. Though the cat was proclaimed a sacred animal in the Fifth and Sixth Egyptian dynasties (2500–2200 B.C.), we have no way of knowing if they were domesticated that early. Most likely, the Egyptians domesticated the cat for pragmatic reasons (to protect their granaries from rodents).

Cretan art depicts the cat as early as 1600 B.C. Cat domestication was subsequently documented in Greece and China (around 500 B.C.), India (100 B.C.), Arabia and Japan (A.D. 600), and Great Britain (A.D. 936).

Willie Morris, in his best-selling book *My Cat Spit McGee* (New York: Viking, 2000), maintains that the first cats in American history were passengers on the *Mayflower* (p. 56). As to their origins, tabby cats and Abyssinians most likely originated in Egypt.

The Persian apparently is a mixture of a number of breeds; however, both the Persian and the Siamese may well have resulted from a domestication of Oriental wild cats.

The Bible mentions the cat not at all; however, it does appear in the apocryphal letter of Jeremiah (Bar. 6:21). Muhammad (A.D. 570–632) is said to have loved his cat so much that he once cut off a piece of his robe rather than awaken it (the *Encyclopedia Britannica,* Fifteenth Edition, 1984; vol. 3, p. 996).

Morris maintains that "About sixty million cats presently live in nearly 30 percent of American households, and pet cats outnumber dogs in the Great Republic by almost two to one" (p. 56).

To live with a cat

Queen Carmen Sylva of Romania ("My Kittens," *Century Magazine,* August 1908) notes that "every one will be surprised when I say that cats are much more faithful and attached than dogs, for this runs counter to the common belief. . . . They never become attached to new masters as easily and quickly as dogs do" (pp. 538, 539).

Why is it that, generally speaking, when we speak of animals we tend to refer to each dog as "he" and to individual cats as "she"? Michael Joseph, in his most insightful cat book, *Cat's Company* (Chicago: Ziff-Davis Publishing Company, 1947), explains it this way: "Even the most ardent cat lover must admit that cats are moody creatures: willful, vain, capricious and changeable. Possibly the fact that most people habitually refer to cats as 'she' is due to the cat's essentially feminine temperament. Therein, I think, lies the secret of the cat's charm. Elusive, subtle, mysterious and graceful, the cat's power of attraction is that of a lovely woman."

And, just as is true with women, one is never home-free. Joseph put it this way: "To win and hold a cat's affection, a process of never-ending courtship is necessary. Cats, like women, will not be taken for granted. They must be admired, petted, coaxed into good humor, played with when they are playful, left to themselves when, as often happens, they prefer to be alone" (p. 54).

They are very territorial, not resting until they have explored every inch of a new residence. And they deeply resent any animal that threatens their supremacy, even a visiting one. Whenever a visitor brought a pet into our home, it took our cat a long time to feel comfortable and secure in the house after the visitor left. How well I remember the case of Smoky. She was accepting of her progeny as long as they were small. We decided to keep one of her kittens, a midnight-black Persian we named Bandit. So violent, filled with jealousy, and downright vicious did Smoky become that she forced us to choose between mother and son. We chose Bandit, and gave Smoky away. In that new home, supreme once more, she again reverted to her former sweet self. As for Bandit, his greatest joy was to hide under a hanging macramé glass-topped

table and pounce upon people's ankles as they walked by. In the middle of the night it was enough to age the half-asleep member of the family five years.

It is true that cats hate to leave the place they call home, but it is rarely true that they love the place more than the people they love. For it breaks their hearts to be left for even a short time. Whenever Queen Carmen Sylva was absent from her palace for a time, as predictable as sunrise, the following occurred upon her return: "I am first reproved and then totally neglected, and no one purrs; they must show me just how unhappy they have been the whole time. I also generally find my door scratched. According to report, the first eight days [after she left] are passed most miserably; after that they sleep from sheer grief, and play not at all" (pp. 540, 541).

And anyone who has tried to sneak away unobserved by a cat knows how tough that is! Instinctively they know you are up to no good and eye the open suitcase with looks that could kill. One of Morris's friends told him, "When I pack my bag I have to hide it, so Bill won't see it. Then I have to sneak out of the house with it. When I come home, he's mad at me. Won't speak to me for a whole day" (p. 24).

Queen Carmen Sylva often took her cats with her on trips. While the cats hated to be wrenched out of their home environment, they hated more being left behind. To almost all cats, home is where those they love most happen to reside.

Cat authorities emphasize the fact that it is almost universal among cats to be fastidiously clean. Joseph declares:

> I have known few cats who did not take their toilet seriously. Mothers wash their babies so often that the importance of personal cleanliness must be apparent to the youngest and most irresponsible kitten. . . . It is an athletic exercise, a pleasant and dignified ceremony, a fine art.
>
> To my Minna Minna Mowbray it was all these things and more. She was the most fastidious of all my cats. After a meal— or, for that matter, after the smallest morsel of food or drink— she would begin the ceremony. There was no undue haste, merely a quiet, efficient preparation for an enjoyable and not-to-

be-disturbed pastime. First, the pink tongue explored the short white fur of the dainty lower jaw, reaching out to apparently inaccessible territory. That active little cat's tongue, no larger than a rosebud's petal, is a marvelous piece of miniature mechanism. Muscular yet supple, thin but strong, the firm pressure of its corrugated surface removes in a moment all traces of the pearly milk drops and crumbs. Not satisfied with merely cleaning up, Minna would elegantly flash her tongue from side to side until the fur glistened.

Then a neatly rounded paw would be raised and moistened. This part of the ceremony was not skipped; the tongue was busily employed for at least a minute, and the moistening process renewed from time to time. Satisfactorily damp, the paw would begin its systematic exploration of whiskers and face. Although no food could possibly have soiled the tortoiseshell patch between her ears, Minna paid it special attention. The ears came next, inside, outside, and behind. Then the glossy tortoiseshell coat and tail must be made even more immaculate.

Finally, and, it seemed, with a sense of climax, the paws themselves. These were extended and stretched in turn, revealing the dark pink protective pads, the curved, delicately strong claws, and the fur-lined crevices between. By this time Minna had got up steam, and the swift but deliberate movement of her indefatigable tongue was a challenge to all the robot machinery of the future.

Satisfied at last, she would indulge in a graceful stretch-and-yawn, and having blinked a grace after meals in my direction the lustrous eyes closed, and Minna would curl herself up for sleep.

And those who know not cats speak disparagingly of "cat-licks"! (pp. 45, 46).

This fastidiousness extends to every aspect of their lives. Most of them shun soiled or pockmarked table or bed coverings of any kind, as well as dishes or

bowls that are anything less than surgically clean. And stale food is anathema to them. For all these reasons and more, cats are rarely sick.

Cats are as individualistic as humans; no mold can possibly fit all. It is said that the ultimate expression of love from a cat is when it licks your face. Queen Carmen Sylva remembers fondly Lilliputt, who

> has such boundless affection for me that she climbs into my
> bosom and continually presses her little forehead against my lips
> for me to kiss. She is so fond of flowers that a potted plant must
> be brought to her every morning: she walks about it, purring,
> smells every bloom, lies down by it, rubs herself against it, and
> repeats the process again and again, purring about the flower
> and caressing it without crumpling a leaf. I have never seen such
> a love of flowers in any other animal; she cannot eat them, and
> finds in them only the purest pleasure. Moreover, she likes only
> flowers which have a pretty color rather than a pleasing odor;
> big red or rose blooms are her special delight (p. 539).

Our daughter, Michelle, has a short-haired black-and-white cat named Joker who has always reveled in the appurtenances found in their bathroom; toilet paper is gleefully unrolled to the fullest extent of the house, and the water in the toilet bowl will be swished until the ecstasy of doing so wanes. Our son, Greg, has a Sylvesterish-looking cat named Spaz. Spaz is so devoted to Greg he'll even wait for him in the hallway when Greg is using the restroom.

Joseph tells of a cat that takes great delight in waiting until the entire family is gathered around the dinner table, and all the victuals are in place, as are vases of flowers, then leaping with one bound to the middle of the table between the vases and daring anyone to remove her. If such attempts are made, she'll make a shambles of food, flowers, and dishes, so she just remains there. "The children, of course, love it" (p. 104).

Cats are never owned in the sense that dogs are. Menacingly threaten a puppy or a dog with a big stick, and most will cower; do the same to the smallest kitten and it will swell up to twice its normal size and snarl and hiss like an infuriated dragon. God could have created us obedient like dogs; instead He created us more like cats—with the power of choice. We have the power within us to either accept or reject Him. And whom does He love most? Strangely enough it is the "prodigal son" who after trying everything else *but* Him, finally comes home. It's the same with us; we love cats because we know they can neither be coerced nor bought. Joseph declares that a cat can no more be domesticated than can a crocodile (p. 1).

Cats are much more independent than dogs—and far less gushy. Early in his career, comedian Bill Cosby recorded an unforgettable monologue about cats and dogs. In it, he postulated that cats come to us only on their terms, not ours. When one of us calls out to a cat, the answer is likely to be, "You rang? Let's see [yawn], let me check my appointment book [turns pages]. Well, I'll be! I do have an opening. But give me a few minutes to check my makeup. I'll be along in a bit." Of course that's one reason kittens and cats are so irresistible—for the same reason we value compliments more from a child than we do from an adult; we know the child's words are from the heart and sincere. That's not an assumption we are as likely to make should an adult say the very same words.

Then there is the psychic dimension. How is it that some cats know exactly when someone they love is returning home? Even if the date for doing so is suddenly changed to another day! And cats are proud, knowing when they are being laughed at, and taking grave offense at it.

Female cats generally have a strongly developed mother instinct. In fact, they have been known to permit puppies, squirrels, marmosets—even mice!—to suckle along with their own. And I recently heard a moving true story about a grieving mother cat whose kittens had been killed. Another mother cat with four kittens carried two of her kittens over to the grieving mother, as much as to say, "There, . . . you can be comforted."

Extremely well developed is their sense of smell. It is with this sense that they find their way home across long distances—often over country unknown to them. Ernest Thompson Seton described this sense metaphorically: "A cat examining carefully the long, invisible, colored stream the wind is made of" (Joseph, p. 130).

In conclusion

Rarely do we humans love dogs and cats equally. For better or worse, both of them are interwoven into the busy lives we lead. One thing is for certain, however: Once a cat comes into your life and casts the feline magic net over you, your life will never be the same again.

I look forward to hearing from you! I always welcome the stories, responses, and suggestions that our readers send. I am putting together collections centered on other genres as well. You may reach me by writing: Joe L. Wheeler, Ph. D., c/o Pacific Press® Publishing Association, P. O. Box 5353, Nampa, ID 83653.

THE UGLIEST CAT IN THE WORLD

-Penny Porter-

A burned clump of charcoal with two great pain-filled eyes—that's all she was, that ugliest cat in the world. But, over time, she became more than that to the people who loved her—far more than that!

* * *

The first time I ever saw Smoky, she was on fire. My three children and I had just arrived at the town dump outside our Arizona desert community to burn our weekly trash. As we approached the smoldering pit, we heard the most mournful cries. A cat was entombed in the smoking rubble below!

Suddenly a large cardboard box, that had been wired shut, burst into flames and exploded. With a long, piercing meow, the animal imprisoned within shot into the air like a flaming rocket and dropped into the ash-filled crater.

"Oh, Mama, do something!" three-year-old Jaymee cried as she and Becky, age six, leaned over the smoking hole.

"It can't possibly still be alive," said Scott. But the ashes moved, and a tiny kitten, charred almost beyond recognition, miraculously struggled to the surface and crawled toward us in agony.

"I'll get her!" Scott yelled. As he stood knee-deep in ashes and wrapped the kitten in my bandanna, I wondered why it didn't cry out from the added pain. Later, we learned we had heard its last meow only moments before.

Back at our ranch, we were doctoring the kitten when my husband, Bill, came in, weary from a long day of mending fences.

"Daddy! We found a burned-up kitty," Jaymee announced. A familiar *Oh, no, not again!* look crossed his face. This wasn't the first time we had greeted him with an injured animal. Though Bill always grumbled, he couldn't bear to see any living creature suffer. So he helped by building cages, perches, pens, and splints for the skunks, rabbits, and birds we brought home. This time was different, however. This was a cat. And Bill, very definitely, did not like cats.

What's more, this was no ordinary cat. Where fur had been, only blisters and a sticky black gum remained. Her ears were gone. Her tail was cooked to the bone. Gone were the claws that would have snatched some unsuspecting mouse. Gone were the little paw pads that would have left telltale tracks on the hoods of our dusty cars and trucks. Nothing that resembled a cat was left—except for two huge cobalt-blue eyes begging for help.

What could we do?

Suddenly I remembered our aloe vera plant and its supposed healing power on burns. So we peeled the leaves, swathed the kitten in slimy aloe strips and gauze bandages, and placed her in Jaymee's Easter basket. All we could see was her tiny face, like a butterfly waiting to emerge from its silk cocoon.

Her tongue was severely burned, and the inside of her mouth was so blistered that she couldn't lap, so we fed her milk and water with an eyedropper. After a while, she began eating by herself.

We named the kitten Smoky.

Three weeks later, the aloe plant was bare. So we coated Smoky with a salve we found; it turned her body a curious shade of green. Not a hair remained, and her tail dropped off. But the children and I adored her. Bill didn't. And Smoky despised him. The reason? He was a pipe smoker, and pipe smokers come armed with matches and butane lighters that flash and burn. Every time Bill lit up,

Smoky panicked, knocking over his coffee cup and lamps before fleeing into the open air duct in the spare bedroom.

"Can't I have any peace around here?" Bill would groan.

In time, Smoky became more tolerant of the pipe and its owner. She'd lie on the sofa and glare at Bill as he puffed away. One day he looked at me and chuckled, "That miserable cat makes me feel guilty."

As Smoky's health improved, we marveled at her patience with the girls, who dressed her in doll clothes and bonnets so the "no ears" wouldn't show. Then they held her up to the mirror so she could see "how pretty" she was.

By the end of her first year, Smoky resembled a well-used welding glove. Scott was now famous among his friends for owning the ugliest pet in the county—probably in the world.

Smoky longed to play outside where the sounds of birds, chickens, and ground squirrels tempted her. When it was time to feed our outdoor pets, including the occasional skunks and assorted lizards, as well as our Mexican lobo, Smoky sat inside, spellbound, with her nose pressed against the window. It was the barn cats, however, that caused her tiny body to tremble with eagerness. But since she had no claws for protection, we couldn't let her go outside unwatched.

Sometimes we took Smoky out on the front porch when other animals weren't around. If she was lucky, an unsuspecting beetle or June bug would make the mistake of strolling across the concrete. Smoky would stalk, bat, and toss the bug until it flipped onto its back where, one hopes, it died of fright before she ate it.

Slowly, oddly, Bill became the one she cared for the most. And before long, I noticed a change in him. He rarely smoked in the house anymore, and one winter night, to my astonishment, I found him sitting in his chair with the leathery little cat curled up on his lap. Before I could say anything, he mumbled curtly, "She's probably cold—no fur, you know."

But Smoky, I reminded myself, liked the cold. Didn't she sleep in front of air ducts and on the cold Mexican tile floor?

Perhaps Bill was starting to like this strange-looking animal just a bit.

Not everyone shared our feelings for Smoky, especially those who had never seen her. Rumors reached a group of self-appointed animal protectors, and one day one of them arrived at our door.

"I've had numerous calls and letters from so many people," the woman said. "They're concerned about a poor little burned-up cat you have in your house. They say," her voice dropped an octave, "she's suffering. Perhaps she should be put out of her misery?"

I was furious. Bill was even more so. "Burned she was," he said, "but suffering? Look for yourself!"

"Here kitty," I called. No Smoky. "She's probably hiding," I said, but our guest didn't answer. When I turned and looked at her, the woman's skin was gray, her mouth hung open, and two fingers pointed. Magnified tenfold in all her naked splendor, Smoky glowered at our visitor from her hiding place behind our 150-gallon aquarium. Instead of the "poor little burned-up suffering creature" the woman expected to see, tyrannosaurus Smoky leered at her through the green aquatic maze. Her open jaws exposed saberlike fangs that glinted menacingly in the neon light. Moments later the woman hurried out the door—smiling now, a little embarrassed and greatly relieved.

During Smoky's second year, a miraculous thing happened. She began growing fur! Tiny white hairs, softer and finer than the down on a chick, gradually grew over three inches long, transforming our ugly little cat into a wispy puff of smoke.

Bill continued to enjoy her company, though the two made an incongruous pair—the big weather-worn rancher driving around with an unlit pipe clenched between his teeth, accompanied by the tiny white ball of fluff. When he got out of the truck to check the cattle, he left the air conditioner on Maximum/Cold for her comfort. Her blue eyes watered, the pink nose ran, but she sat there, unblinking, in ecstasy. Other times, he picked her up and, holding her close against his denim jacket, took her along when he left the truck.

Smoky was three years old on the day she went with Bill to look for a missing calf. Searching for hours, he would leave the truck door open when he got out to look. The pastures were parched and crisp with dried grasses and tumbleweed. A storm loomed on the horizon, and still no calf. Discouraged, without thinking, Bill reached into his pocket for his lighter and spun the wheel. A spark shot to the ground, and, in seconds, the field was on fire.

Frantic, Bill didn't think about the cat. Only after the fire was under control and the calf found did he return home—and remember.

"Smoky!" he cried. "She must have jumped out of the truck! Did she come home?"

No. And we knew she'd never find her way home from two miles away. To make matters worse, it had started to rain so hard we couldn't go out to look for her.

Bill was distraught, blaming himself. We spent the next day searching, wishing she could meow for help, and knowing she'd be helpless against predators. It was no use.

Two weeks later Smoky still wasn't home. We were afraid she was dead by now, for the rainy season had begun, and the hawks, wolves, and coyotes had families to feed.

Then came the biggest rainstorm our region had had in fifty years. By morning, flood waters stretched for miles, marooning wildlife and cattle on scattered islands of higher ground. Frightened rabbits, raccoons, squirrels, and desert rats waited for the water to subside, while Bill and Scott waded knee-deep, carrying bawling calves back to their mamas and safety.

The girls and I were watching intently when suddenly Jaymee shouted, "Daddy! There's a poor little rabbit over there. Can you get it?"

Bill waded to the spot where the animal lay, but when he reached out to help the tiny creature, it seemed to shrink back in fear. "I don't believe it," Bill cried. "It's Smoky!" His voice broke. "Little Smoky!"

My eyes ached with tears when that pathetic little cat crawled into the outstretched hands of the man she had grown to love. He pressed her shivering body to his chest, talked to her softly, and gently wiped the mud from her face. All the while her blue eyes fastened on his with unspoken understanding. He was forgiven.

Smoky came home again. The patience she showed as we shampooed her astounded us. We fed her scrambled eggs and ice cream, and to our joy she seemed to get well.

But Smoky had never really been strong. One morning when she was barely four years old, we found her limp in Bill's chair. Her heart had simply stopped.

As I wrapped her tiny body in one of Bill's red neckerchiefs and placed her in a child's shoe box, I thought about the many things our precious Smoky had taught us—things about trust, affection, and struggling against the odds when everything says you can't win. She reminded us that it's not what's outside that counts; it's what's inside, deep in our hearts.

That's why Smoky will always be in my heart. And why, to me, she will always be the most beautiful cat in the world.

* * * * *

"The Ugliest Cat in the World," by Penny Porter. Published April 1984 in Reader's Digest *and in Porter's anthology,* Heartstrings and Tail-Tuggers *(Ravenhawk Books, 1999). Reprinted by permission of the author.* Reader's Digest *has published more of Penny Porter's true-life animal stories than those of any other author. Today, she lives and writes from her home in Tucson, Arizona.*

THREE C'S FOR COMFORT

-Joseph Leininger Wheeler-

I had heard about the mysterious black cat long before I met him. Quite frankly, I found the story mighty hard to believe. Until . . .

* * *

On an August day of 2004, a sorrowful woman stood next to her car in the parking lot of Callahan Court, a Roseburg, Oregon, facility for individuals afflicted with Alzheimer's and dementia. Suddenly, a wretched-looking scraggly black cat appeared out of nowhere and leaped onto the hood of the car. Then he gently approached the woman with love and empathy in his eyes. He seemed to know what she was going through. Ignoring the cat's disreputable condition, she gathered him in her arms and rained tears down onto his matted fur.

Ask anyone about the worst possible nightmare where aging is concerned, and almost certainly it would be one's mind going before one's body. Alzheimer's and other forms of dementia strip an individual of selfhood, memory, and awareness, leaving behind only a shell—a person who looks like the person you have always loved, but when you look into the once welcoming eyes, you discover that there is no longer anyone home. A stranger lives there now, a stranger who is puzzled as to who you are and why you are there.

Now, the grieving woman, solaced after a time, lowered the cat, stroked him, and returned through two sets of double doors to her dying mother inside. Hour after interminable hour, she sat there by the bed holding on to that unresponsive hand and looking into those unresponsive eyes. Whenever she'd escape the tension of the room, outside, on the hood of her car, would be that black cat, waiting to comfort her.

Days passed. Still the emaciated cat faithfully kept its vigil on the hood of her car. No one knew where the cat came from or if there was an owner who claimed him. One thing was all too clear: No one either fed him or gave him anything to drink—yet he somehow managed to stay alive.

Three days later, after it was over at last, the daughter blindly stumbled through the entryway to the parking lot. Still waiting for her was the cat. She scooped him up and held him for a long time, he being the only family she had to share the moment with. After a while she re-entered Callahan Court—only with the cat. But when she reached the room that had held her mother for so long, she couldn't bear to go in. It was here that the kindly administrator, Freda Smith, found her: weeping convulsively, the cat in her arms.

When she finally recovered her composure to some extent, she told Freda the story of the past few days, then importuned her, "Wouldn't you please let this cat stay here? Without him, I don't know how I could have made it through."

Freda looked at the pitiful specimen of cathood and had grave misgivings. What would people say? A cat—and such a miserable looking specimen as this!—being given entrée to the facility they worked so hard to keep clean, sanitary, and cheerful! The daughter, studying Freda's unconvinced face, acknowledged temporary defeat and left.

Freda wondered if she had done the right thing.

Several days later, the woman returned, still with the cat. But what a difference! It hardly looked like the same animal. The cat had obviously been well fed in the interim.

He had been cleaned up, the matted fur had been snipped out; and he had been brushed until the fur almost had a glow to it. Furthermore, the cat had been given a complete physical, along with a battery of shots. He now had a clean bill of health, and it showed.

The woman pleaded, *"Now,* can he stay? His place is here—here where he can comfort other grieving ones like me. I'll even help pay for his upkeep—*Please?* Won't you at least give him a chance?"

What could Freda say?

The cat stayed.

The Comforter

It didn't take long for the newest arrival to make his presence known. He would make his rounds, supremely self-assured, and permit his now fastidious self to be held and stroked. Everyone, it seemed, whether caretakers or care-recipients, had something to say to him. When ready to go outdoors to answer nature's call, he would wait by the exit doors until someone opened them for him. Same pattern for re-entry.

No one knew what to call him so, more or less by default, he became known as C.C.C. for "Callahan Court Cat"—C.C. for short, because people soon tired of having to say "C" three times when they were calling to him.

He ruled supreme. A big yellow cat was in the habit of hanging around looking for handouts. C.C. would tolerate no interlopers. Fierce battles took place before the yellow cat saw fit to panhandle elsewhere.

Occasionally, C.C. would bring mice (usually still alive) to the front door, just to let everyone know he was earning his keep.

He loved to swat pencils and pens off Freda's desk.

But what has never ceased to amaze the Callahan Court staff is how C.C. instinctively knows when the end is drawing near for any of his family. Those who gather in various rooms while another life ebbs to its close would look up to see a fellow sympathizer and mourner, appropriately attired in black fur, coming through the doorway. Once there, he would remain hour after hour, offering quiet companionship and comfort. No one ever had to bring this mourner in:

Instinctively, he *knew.* Knew the difference between "just another day" and *The* day.

And so C.C. became a legend.

We Meet C.C.

My sister Marji phoned us and told us that for Mom, the end was near. For more than four years, the mother we had known for so long had been withdrawing from us. Not of her own accord—but rudely escorted by that puzzling disease called dementia. Three of those years had been spent in Callahan Court. At first, Mom had been able to feed herself; later, that skill left her, so she had to be fed by others.

But now Mom had determined to go home to her God. Gently but firmly, she now pushed away all attempts to feed her or help her drink. She had always told us, "When I go, I want to go quickly and under my own power, while I still have all my marbles."

Though she was not granted that wish, deep in the layers of awareness that remained, she summoned the power to carry out the intent of her Living Will.

My wife, Connie, and I flew out to join my sister at Mom's bedside. Those who work at Callahan Court are indeed a breed apart. Once, during one of my many visits, I sighed to one of them, "Oh, I wish you could have known Mom before!" I was going to tell her about my mother's once phenomenal near photographic memory, her elocutionary powers (she could hold an audience in the palm of her hand, veering between laughter and tears) as she recited and emoted stories, readings, and poetry—all by memory, leaving her listeners limp at the end. I was going to tell her about the hundreds of children, all over the Americas, whose education she supported or raised money for. Oh, there was so much I was going to tell her . . . but my listener only smiled and gently clasped my arm, saying softly, "But see, we don't need to know that mother you once knew: We love her as she is *now.*" I could tell that she did, that everyone working there did. Here were all these aged people with withered bodies and wandering minds—unlovely to the casual observer, unpredictable in what they'd do or say. "Second childhood," we've always called it, when certain aged people revert to childish ways and childish speech—but, without the childish beauty and rapidly expanding minds that make children so enchanting. Yet, those who work at Callahan Court not only love each one, they respect each one, and dwell on the vestiges of personality and uniqueness that yet remain.

One way their care is evidenced is by the way they keep their charges clean and neat. There is no unpleasant smell assailing you when you walk in. You know almost instantly that this is a home where all are loved and cherished—and thus deserving of C.C.

As for Mom, during the last few days of her life that we were with her, only twice did I feel she knew we were there—and only for milliseconds. Each night, we expected it to be her last, but come next morning, there she'd be: a little weaker, but still holding on to life. How incredibly strong the spirit in that tiny form of barely eighty pounds!

On the third day, into our room came the resident mourner. C.C. stopped at Mom's bedside, then paid his respects to Marji and Connie before moving on to me, looking up at me, letting me know I was not alone in my grief. I picked him up, and there on my lap he stayed, for several hours. After a time, he left me, walked over to Mom's bed, jumped up on it, and stretched out against her ominously unmoving legs, and remained there lovingly nestled against her for a number of hours. C.C. brought serenity into the room just by that act. Once C.C. left the room, but soon returned to his vigil. The Callahan staff looked knowingly at each other, as though to say, *Can't be long now—C.C.'s been in there all day!* As for us in the room: Connie, Marji, C.C., and me, we were a sacred circle of four.

Next morning, as if on signal, in came the staff, one by one. Each quietly slipping into the room to say goodbye to a later woman we children had not known very well; to a woman they considered gentle, considerate, and beautiful; to a smile that never left until the very last days. Though they had not known our mother long, they loved her deeply, and thus grieved at her passing. Some of them returned again and again. Somehow, even in her much diminished state, Mom had made a major impact on all these lives.

The folks with Hospice came. The chaplain told us, "It would be well if you spoke with your mother and prayed with her one last time. Open up your heart to her. I've seen it happen again and again: Somehow they tend to wait until words from those they have loved longest penetrate their layers of awareness, words bringing the reassurance that they are loved and cherished, and that it's OK to go."

So I did. I held her unresponsive hand, and told her she'd been a wonderful mother, and that we all loved and cherished her. We would always do so. I prayed for her and those in the room. Then I told her it was all right if she wanted to go home. Marji followed with the same reassurances. Then I felt a shudder go through Mom, followed by a relaxing of her muscles, and a slowing of her breathing. Within fifteen minutes, her spirit returned to the God who gave it.

* * * * *

Afterwards, as the women prepared Mom for burial, I left the room and sank down into a comfortable lounge chair in the foyer. And held C.C. Staff members passing by would pause, smile, or wipe away a tear, and move on.

And I? Just like the grieving daughter of last August, I rained tears onto my comforter: C.C., the cat whom God sent out of nowhere to bring solace to Callahan Court.

THANKFUL CATS

-Abbie Farwell Brown-

Bob and Betty were anticipating Thanksgiving as usual—until their mother made a rather strange observation.

* * *

Bob and Betty were much excited about Thanksgiving. It seemed a long time since the last one, which they remembered with enthusiasm. Such a bevy of engaging uncles and aunts from distant corners of the land! Such joking and laughing and merry stories at the dinner table! Such monster turkeys and heaps of goodies—more than anyone, even Bob, could possibly eat!

"It's tomorrow!" said Bob exultantly. "Only one more day to wait, and then— my!" He smacked his lips and patted the buttons of his jacket affectionately.

"Bob!" exclaimed his mother, who overheard him. "Have you forgotten what Thanksgiving means? It isn't just eating more than is good for you, is it?"

"I don't know," said Bob doubtfully.

"What is it, Mama?" asked Betty, who was younger than Bob.

"It's a time to be thankful for all the good things we have, Dear," said her mother.

"Well, I'll be thankful after dinner," said Bob.

"Must everybody be thankful?" asked Betty. "I'd guess some people don't have anything to be thankful for."

"Don't they have any turkey?" asked Bob, sympathetically.

"That's the sad part," said Mama. "But if we all pitch in and do kind things for other people on Thanksgiving Day, then surely everyone would have something to be thankful for. That would be the very best way to keep Thanksgiving."

The kitchen was full of pleasant odors, which excited Pete, the white kitten, just as they excited Bob and Betty. Pete wandered restlessly about mewing like a little beggar until Katie, the cook, said, "You children, do take that little beast away from under my feet! Leave my kitchen, will you? I can't cook at all with a mess of children and cats teasing all the time."

"Pete is thinking about his Thanksgiving dinner," said Betty, taking the kitten up in her arms and carrying him to the playroom. "Petey, dear, you're thankful, aren't you? You ought to be! Just think of all the little kittens who are not going to have a single turkey bone to chew on tomorrow. And think of all the poor lost cats who haven't any warm fire to sit by and nobody to play with them!"

"There's one of them now," said Bob, who was looking out of the window. A thin, forlorn cat was creeping along the back fence. Finally, it disappeared into the back alley.

"Oh, Bob!" cried Betty, struck by a sudden idea. "We haven't done anything to help anybody this Thanksgiving. Why couldn't we help *them?*"

"Help what?" asked Bob.

"Why, the hungry cats," answered Betty. "There will be ever so many more scraps left from dinner tomorrow than Pete can eat. Let's ask Mama if we can take them out to some other poor lost cats who have no dinner at all."

"All right," said Bob. "Let's ask her." And they did.

Mrs. James had no objection to their plan. Indeed, she thought it a splendid one, and told Katie to save all the turkey bones after Thanksgiving dinner for the children's charity—all, of course, except a good plateful for little Pete.

But, meantime, Bob had another idea. "We might as well make a *lot* of thankful cats while we're about it," he said. "I know there are heaps of them around here. Let's ask some of the neighbors to save us their turkey bones, too."

Betty agreed. So the children called at the houses of several people whom they knew very well and told them what they wanted. Everybody seemed to think it a funny idea; but it wasn't funny to Bob and Betty. But, since each neighbor promised to contribute to the cats' Thanksgiving, it didn't matter how much they laughed.

Thanksgiving Day came, and my! What a good time they had at the Jameses' house. Bob and Betty were very thankful, indeed. Pete was still crunching his dish of bones thankfully when Bob and Betty filled a basket with all the good things

that Katie had saved for them, and started on their errand.

"We had better take the big wagon," said Bob. "Then we can easily collect all the neighbors' bones." They then dragged the cart down the alley, and stopped at the doors of their

friends' houses for the packages that were ready for them.

"I feel just like a City Wagon!" chuckled Bob, as they left the last house.

"I feel like a Children's Mission," said Betty, solemnly. "Oh, Bob! Look! There's the first cat!"

Sure enough. There in the gutter crouched the most forlorn and desperate looking cat you ever saw. Her fur was all draggled and dirty, and her sides were so thin that they almost touched. She looked at the children with frightened eyes and started to run away.

"Poor kitty!" cried Betty, stooping low and holding out her hand caressingly. "Don't go away. We've come to make you thankful!"

Bob picked out some appetizing bones and gently approached the cat.

"Just smell this!" he said. The cat, who was creeping away, suddenly pricked up her ears and began to sniff. Then, trembling with excitement, she snatched at the bones and began to eat ravenously. Bob and Betty gave her a generous supply.

"We mustn't stop to watch her finish," said Bob. "There are so many other hungry cats waiting."

The next cat they met was a big gray Tom, who was mewing sadly on the pavement. Someone had just driven him away from a window where he had been sniffing at tempting Thanksgiving odors. You should have seen Tom's grin of delight when the children set his Thanksgiving dinner before him! He did not eat like a gentleman, poor Tom, but he was certainly very thankful!

They left him and went on to the next corner. At first, they thought there was nothing down this alley. But suddenly they spied something dark moving about, and in another minute a cat ran up the fence in front of them. It was a poor, thin mother cat. And there at the foot of the fence crouched her two kittens. They were dear little things; one was black, and one was yellow—but they were very thin and wretched looking. They tried to run away when Bob and Betty approached. But there was nowhere to go, so they crouched, trembling, frightened almost to death. The poor mother cat ran back and forth along the fence, afraid to leave her babies and equally afraid to come nearer. Bob stooped and took up one of the kittens in his arms. "Poor little things!" he said. "Oh, Betty, I'm afraid they are too small to eat turkey."

"Can't we get them some milk?" asked Betty anxiously. "I have two cents, Bob!"

Bob fumbled in his pockets. "I have four," he said. "I'll go and see how much milk I can get for six cents." He left Betty to watch the express wagon and get acquainted with the kittens while he ran to the little bake shop on the corner, which luckily was open, though it was a holiday—for the baker lived in the rooms behind his shop.

When Bob told what he wanted, the man grinned, as everybody did.

"Well! Well!" he said. "Six cents! Hmm. That ain't much. But I'll let you have a quart for your cats. It's a pity they should go hungry on Thanksgiving Day."

The kind man also let Bob have a cracked saucer for the kittens' milk. Bob ran back to Betty with his treasures. "Here it is!" he cried joyously. "Now, we'll make the kittens thankful!"

Betty had made friends with the two kittens, and they were soon lapping their milk eagerly. The mother cat was still timid. She watched the children anxiously.

"Come down, poor mama kitty, and join the Thanksgiving party!" said Betty, holding out her arms to the cat. Bob spread out a tempting pile of scraps.

"Me-ow!" wailed the hungry cat. She looked and looked, yearned and yearned. Finally, she could bear it no longer. She leaped off the fence, rushed to the bowl, and was soon devouring the tempting morsels. Evidently the poor thing had not enjoyed a square meal for many days.

Bob and Betty left that happy family reluctantly and moved on. But I cannot begin to tell all the things that happened in the next hour. Who would have guessed there were so many poor hungry cats in the world? Many times Betty's, and even Bob's, eyes filled with tears at what they saw. But the cart of turkey bones and the can of milk lasted for a long time—and left behind a score or more of thankful cats in different dark corners of that neighborhood.

On the way home the children stopped at the kind baker's to leave the can and the saucer. "Well, did you find many dinnerless cats?" asked the man. The children told him everything. When they came to the part about the old cat and the kittens, he asked, "What color were them kits?"

They told him one was black and one was yellow. "Well," said the man, "if you find them again you may bring them here. I need a cat to keep the rats away. And I do admire black and yellow kits!"

You can imagine how fast Bob and Betty ran back to the alley. Sure enough, the old cat and her babies were still there, licking their paws thankfully after their good dinner. And this time they were not afraid, but came purring to meet the children. Bob took the old cat in his arms, and Betty carried the two kittens, as they made their way once again to the baker's shop. The man received them warmly. So this cat family had reason to be very grateful, indeed, on that Thanksgiving Day, for they now had a good home and a kind master. The baker said that he was thankful, too.

Bob and Betty came home tired and happy. "It has been the nicest Thanksgiving Day I ever knew!" said Betty.

"Yes," said Bob. "It makes me thankfuller than I ever was before, when I think of all those thankful cats."

* * * * *

"Thankful Cats," by Abbie Farwell Brown. Published November 23, 1907, in The Churchman. *Text reprinted by permission of Joe Wheeler (P.O. Box 1246, Conifer, CO 80433). Abbie Farwell Brown is considered to be one of America's foremost writers of stories and books during the first third of the twentieth century. She is best known for books such as* The Lonesomest Doll, The Christmas Angel, *and* A Pocketful of Posies.

SMALL THINGS

-Margaret E. Sangster, Jr.-

The doctor was tired and out of sorts. He said things—things that cut like knives. Just like that, it was all over between them.
All over . . . until . . .

* * *

Evie was trimming the Christmas tree. She was trimming it with tinsel and glass balls and imitation icicles. She was fastening a chubby small angel on the topmost branch when the doctor came in.

"Hello, darling," she called, peering down at him through a green barricade of branches (for the tree was tall, and Evie was standing on a little red ladder). "Hello, darling! Isn't this a swell angel!"

The doctor took off his fur-lined gloves and rubbed his hands together. He had been driving, and it was very cold—considerably colder than the usual December.

"No," he said, and his voice was as chill as the weather outside. "No, I don't like the angel. It's—it's too fat. It's obese. It looks like a kewpie."

Evie pouted. "I'm too fat myself," she said. "Christmas—and Christmas candy—has wrecked me, already. Maybe I look like a kewpie, a trifle, myself! And yet—you like *me*."

"I'm engaged to you," said the doctor, "so it goes without saying that I like you . . ."

"Usually it does!" murmured Evie.

"And," the doctor continued, ignoring the interruption, "and you're grown up. You're not little. I hate little things."

"I'm not very tall," said Evie. Morosely she began to clamber down the steps of the red ladder.

"That wasn't what I meant," said the doctor. "You're not tall—no. But you're an adult. That fool angel isn't. It looks like a baby I brought into the world this afternoon. An emergency Caesarean, it was. The mother was an Italian; it was her fifth child in five years. A nasty, fat little baby."

Evie was all at once crouched down in front of the doctor. "Tell me about it," she begged. "Darling, tell me all about it. Just think, born on the afternoon before Christmas! What a break for a baby."

The doctor snorted.

"I'm not an obstetrician," he said. "It isn't my business, seeing that babies are born—on the afternoon before Christmas or any afternoon. If all of the other doctors in the world weren't off at strange places for the holidays, I'd

have told her to go somewhere else for her Caesarean. But there wasn't any alternative!"

"Don't you . . ." Evie's eyes were suddenly round in her round little face, "don't you like babies, Ned? Or are you only having fun with me? Say you're only having fun! Because it . . . it isn't nice, this sort of pretend."

"Nice, my hat!" said the doctor. "I was the oldest of nine children. We were poor as mud. I saw my mother falter and fade and die under the burden of nine mouths to feed! Baby mouths, always open, always squalling! I worked for them—to keep them full, those mouths—when I was only a kid myself. Selling papers, printer's devil, running errands, everything. Snatched an education catch as catch can. I'd be a really great surgeon, today, Evie, instead of a middling one, if I hadn't wasted so much time on the flock of them."

"Wasted?" queried Evie very softly.

"*Wasted!*" said the doctor savagely.

There was silence for a moment while snow beat with white insistent fingers against the window pane. A fire danced on the hearth. Evie tried, rather unsuccessfully, to braid her plump, small fingers. Then . . .

"If we had babies, Ned," she asked softly, "you wouldn't mind it, would you? Keeping their little mouths full, I mean? You wouldn't even mind, would you, if there were nine of them? They couldn't all be babies at the same time!"

"There won't be nine of them," said the doctor. Curiously his eyes watched Evie's fingers, lacing and unlacing. "There won't be any babies, Evie, if I can help it! I've had babies enough in my life. I'm cured. I wish . . ." his tone was petulant; the emergency operation had been a difficult one. "I wish that you'd keep your hands still. I've a headache, and it makes me nervous."

Evie's fingers were strangely quiet for a moment. So, for that matter, was Evie. And then, with a sudden swift movement, the fingers were no longer quiet. The fingers of the right hand were very busy removing a ring—a ring that sparkled in the firelight—from one of the fingers of the left hand.

"I'm afraid," said Evie—and it didn't sound like her voice, even to herself— "I'm afraid that I'll make you nervous, Ned, always and always. I'm . . ." she was dropping the ring into one of the doctor's hands, "I'm sorry!"

The doctor hadn't been expecting the ring. It slipped between his fingers and lay on the rug. It was as bright, lying there, as a tear.

"For crying out loud," said the doctor, "what are you getting at, Evie? Do you mean that you are . . ."

"I'm breaking our engagement!" answered Evie.

The doctor should have taken her into his arms and kissed her, just then. He should have picked up the ring and forced it back upon the proper one of Evie's fingers. But he wasn't that sort.

"I thought you loved me!" he said stiffly, instead.

"I thought I did," answered Evie. She was looking past him. "But I guess I don't. Not as much as I love babies . . . and fat little angels . . . and other small things."

The doctor was rising swiftly. How was Evie to know that his head was all one throb and that the tears were very close to his eyes?

"Then, it's goodbye?" he asked dully.

"It's goodbye!" agreed Evie.

She turned back to the tree and started unsteadily to mount the little red ladder.

The doctor drew on his fur-lined gloves, put on his great coat, and reached for his hat. He didn't speak again, neither did he stoop to retrieve the glimmering ring. He only walked out of Evie's living room and out of Evie's apartment and out of Evie's life. He only climbed into his waiting car and started, mechanically, to drive downtown—through the blurring, blinding snow storm—toward his own apartment. As he went along the great avenue, he passed parks, each with its Christmas tree—they were like Evie's tree, magnified—and church yards, each with its tree, too. Over the door of one church hung a huge electric sign. In green and red lights, it spelled out: "Good will toward men."

Seeing it, the doctor muttered something beneath his breath.

* * *

The day seemed too grim to be the afternoon before Christmas. As the doctor drove along the avenue he told himself that it was just the sort of day on which to get unengaged!

The snow looked gray instead of white—for it was very close to evening. The arc lights, already blazing, made shallow paths across its grayness. People, hurrying to and fro, were black, distorted shapes in the general gloom, like gnomes. There wasn't any shine to the eastern sky. There wasn't even the faintest hint of a star.

"I'm dog tired," the doctor told himself as he drove. "Maybe I'm asleep, already—and having a nightmare. This isn't happening to me!" (He loved Evie, you see—pretty, plump Evie—very much indeed!) "It's happening," he laughed painfully, "to a couple of other fellows . . ."

There wasn't any shine in the eastern sky. Even the light from the street lamps looked dirty! The doctor swung off the avenue and drove through the sedate brownstone-housed street on which he lived. He drew up in front of the old-fashioned, high-stooped place that was his home. It had been converted into apartments, that home. His apartment was on the ground floor.

"Thank God," he said wearily, "that I've no long flights of stairs to climb this night." And then, "I won't even take my car into the garage. It can stand in front until morning, and freeze . . ."

Stiffly he climbed out of the car. Achingly he closed the car's door, and locked it. And then, fumbling in his pocket for his keys, he mounted the steps of the high stoop. Perhaps it was the snow beating into his face that made him feel so suddenly blind. Perhaps it was something else. Perhaps . . .

The doctor uttered a sharp exclamation—and paused, as sharply, in his upward climb. That dark blob on his doormat—he'd thought it was only a shadow, at first. He hadn't known until it cried that it was alive. He'd almost stepped on it!

"For the love of . . ." he began.

The blob upon the doormat lifted a furry black blot of a face and uttered a feeble complaint. It did more than lift its face; it lifted an infinitesimal black paw. The doctor saw that the paw was twisted oddly, unnaturally.

"A compound fracture, at least," he heard himself saying foolishly, before he realized that the black blob, after all, was only a kitten.

A stray kitten come to his doorstep from some grim, never-never land. A kitten that lifted its tiny, snow-drenched head and sobbed out its babyish woe. Sobbed out the agony and fear and lack of understanding that touches the soul of every homeless animal.

The doctor, his arms hanging limply at his sides, looked down at the forlorn little creature.

I should kick it off the porch, he thought savagely, adding aloud, "the hateful, whining little beast." Suddenly all of his own agony and fear and lack of understanding were crystallized in this miserable bit of black fur. "You're the reason for it all," he shouted down at the kitten. "You and . . . and things like you! If it weren't for you I'd still be engaged. I'd . . ."

The kitten, gathering all of its forces, struggled to three small feet. It limped piteously across the doormat. It crept agonizingly toward the doctor. It rubbed feebly against his trouser leg.

"Oh, no!" said the doctor. Stooping, he lifted the kitten into the curve of his arm. He held it gingerly, but even so he could tell that it was the thinnest kitten in the whole world! "Oh, goodness!" said the doctor. "Even a kitten's got a right to die indoors on the night before Christmas!"

* * *

After all, it *was* nearly dead! And it wasn't a human being, either—it was only an animal. The doctor didn't know much about pets; he'd never had a pet, even when he was a boy. You see, he'd never, really, been a boy. But there was one thing that he did know—even when he was utterly spent, both of body and of soul. He knew surgery. He knew when a leg, even the leg of a worthless kitten, was all out of line. And he knew what should be done to make it assume proper proportions.

"If it were a horse," he said, as he unlocked the front door, crossed the general hall, and unlocked his apartment door, "if it were a horse I'd found on my doorstep" (the idea of a horse on his doorstep didn't seem remotely funny just then to the doctor!), "a horse with a broken leg, I'd call a policeman. And the policeman would come and shoot it and put it out of its misery! But," the doc-

tor switched on the lights in his living room, "but one can't call a policeman to shoot a kitten!"

It was as if the kitten understood. For, blinking against the sudden glare of light, the kitten tucked his head into the hollow of the doctor's elbow and tried very feebly to purr.

"He's got guts, anyway," said the doctor. And then all at once he reached for his handkerchief. "Oh, Evie!" said the doctor, and blew his nose violently. "Oh, Evie, my dear . . ."

The kitten snuggled closer. The purr was more feeble than it had been. Gingerly, the doctor ran his finger along the bone that rose aggressively high on the kitten's spine.

"Probably," said the doctor, "he's dying, now. But I'll get him some milk, anyway."

He carried the kitten carefully in the direction of his minute kitchenette. "After all, it's bad enough to die, but to die hungry . . ."

Oddly, the doctor found himself wondering whether, years from now, he himself would die hungry. *Heart hungry.*

There was milk in the kitchenette. The maid who came mornings to tidy up had forgotten to put it in the refrigerator, and for once the doctor was grateful for her carelessness. The milk wouldn't be clammy; it wouldn't be necessary to heat it. Still holding the kitten, he poured some of the milk, clumsily, into a cereal dish. Still holding the kitten, he thrust the dish under its nose.

"Drink that!" he commanded harshly. "You little pest!"

The kitten pushed its nose down into the saucer of milk. The doctor could feel the quiver of its desperate eagerness. Once, when he was an intern, he had treated a starvation case; he knew the symptoms.

"Slowly, there," he said to the kitten, "don't go so fast . . ." He held the saucer away for a moment, waited until the kitten breathed more normally, and held it back again under the quivering nose. After a while the kitten drank more quietly, and under its drying fur the doctor could feel its little sides growing puffy. When finally the saucer was empty, it raised a small face very daubed with milk. And then with a supreme effort, it lifted its well paw and began weakly to wash the milk from its face.

It was the effort back of that instinctive cleaning that decided the doctor—that decided him, for better or for worse.

"A gentleman like you," said the doctor, "deserves two paws to wash with!"

With something like respect in the line of his mouth, in the expression of his eyes, he carried the sated kitten back to the living room. There was a broad mahogany table in the living room; it held books, and copies of the *A.M.A. Journal,* and Evie's picture in a white jade frame. The doctor removed the books and the magazines, and in their place he put a flat cushion from one of the chairs. But Evie's picture he didn't move.

"Maybe," he said to the picture, "maybe you'd like me better if you could see me do something I'm really good at!"

He laid the kitten on the cushion and went into the bathroom for his emergency kit and some towels. The doctor had his office in a hospital; he hadn't much equipment at home! But he had enough, quite enough, to take care of the needs of a kitten!

Gently carrying his emergency case, he came back to the living room and his patient. The patient was drowsing—the triple result of food, warmth, and pain. With fingers surprisingly tender—for they were very large—he took the kitten's injured paw in his hand and parted the fur. The kitten stirred and whimpered, but he didn't scratch. It seemed to know.

"Whew!" said the doctor, surveying the paw. Not only was it broken, it was mangled. It looked as if it had been chewed. It might have been!

"Amputation!" said the doctor.

There was ether in the emergency case. There just happened to be. The doctor went into the bathroom again for cotton and a medicine dropper. On the way back he asked himself, *Why not put it to sleep—permanently? Life's hard enough for whole things, let alone maimed!*

But then he met Evie's pictured eyes smiling at him from out of their chaste white jade frame. And at almost the same moment he remembered how the kitten had washed its face with one paw.

"I'll show you, honey," he found himself saying wildly to the picture (he'd never called Evie anything like that to her face), "and I won't amputate, either! *It can be done!*"

Little by little, with the aid of the cotton and the medicine dropper, the doctor put the little kitten to sleep. It lay very limp and soft—its fur had dried longer than most kitten fur, and fluffier—under his hand. Then very tenderly—much more tenderly than he had worked the week before upon the shin bone of a multimillionaire—he began to operate upon a thing so tiny that it might have been a smudge of ink. A thing so broken that God Himself, who watches over sparrows, must have known pity!

It wasn't an easy operation. It took a long while. Once, briefly, the doctor looked up from his task and sighed and met Evie's watchful gaze. And . . .

"The patient was on the operating table," he said to her picture, "for a matter of hours." It was the closest the doctor had ever come to being whimsical!

At last the operation was over, and the sad little paw—miraculously fitted together into some semblance of proper mechanics—was held together with splints made of those wooden things that physicians put upon your tongue when they ask you to say "ahh." And over the splints was wound a white, firm, tidy bandage that looked extremely professional—and smelt so, too.

"And that," said the doctor, "is that!"

The kitten stirred, ever so slightly, but it wasn't ready yet to come out of the ether. It had had quite a lot of ether for a kitten. The doctor, seeing it move, looked at his wrist watch. The kitten's movement had been very sleepy.

"My word!" he said, for it was very late, indeed. *"My word!"*

No use now to think about dinner. The restaurant down the street, where he so often ate when he was alone, would be closed. But there was still milk in the kitchenette and probably bread, too. Bread and milk were good enough for anyone.

But as he was eating the bread and milk from out of a deep bowl, the doctor was remembering a telephone conversation that he'd had that morning with Evie.

"We'll have our dinner at my place tonight," she had said. "Believe it or not, I'm going to cook it. It will be a goose."

The doctor wondered whether Evie was eating her goose alone.

"You can't have your goose and eat it, too!" he found himself saying, and wondered seriously if he had gone mad! Perhaps he had. Perhaps this major operation that he had just performed on such a minor part of life was only one of the delusions that went with madness. Just to make himself feel sane, he ate a second bowl of bread and milk, although he didn't really want it. It didn't make him feel sane, either—just stuffy!

And the kitten wasn't a delusion. For as the doctor left the kitchenette and wended his way toward the living room, he heard sounds of the kitten. Sounds of utter, racking distress.

"How could I have been such a fool," the doctor questioned as he broke into a trot, "all that ether on top of all that milk! *No wonder!*"

For the kitten was being violently, dreadfully sick at its tummy. It had come out of the ether and had started all over again to taste the bitterness of existence. It raised sad eyes in a peaked black face to the man who had tried so hard to save its life. And then its eyes rolled back strangely and a convulsive shudder took its little body into a dreadful, wrenching paroxysm.

The doctor stood beside the table looking down, dazedly, at the kitten. For a moment he stood there and then he was galvanized into action. He picked up the little thing swiftly in his clever hands and was forcing open the tiny, rigid mouth.

"Oh, no, you don't!" he said, and his voice was half a sob. "Oh, no, you won't! Not *now*. I won't let you die. Not after bringing you through the hardest operation I've ever done!"

The rigid little mouth was open now. Into it the doctor was dropping a brown liquid—not much, just a little—from a slim vial in his emergency box. The tremors with which the little body had been shaken began to pass. Two beady kitten eyes rolled back to normal. And the doctor found that he was wiping beads of sweat from his own forehead.

"You—*kitten!*" he said softly. "Don't you let me catch you acting up again! Don't you dare," his voice broke on a high note.

But the little kitten—oh, it wasn't that the little kitten didn't want to mind. Only he'd had rather a bad time of it. Cold, privation, hunger, racking agony,

anesthetics . . . he'd hardly been old enough to know so many sensations, really!

All through the night—the night before Christmas—the doctor fought for a little kitten's life, a life that hung by a black little thread! Fought for that—and for something else. Fought for the rebirth of love in the pictured eyes of a girl. Fought for a rebirth of tenderness. He fought with patient, prayerful hands, and with slim, sharp instruments. He fought with hot compresses and ice packs. He fought, toward dawn, with a stimulant and hot milk. He didn't know that the room was chill with the chill that comes before sunup. He didn't know that it had stopped snowing. He didn't know, even, that it was Christmas Day. He only knew—when a tired little kitten thrust out a wee, pinkish tongue to lick his fingers—that he had won a victory out of all proportions to the life of a small animal.

"Well," he said almost languidly, as the kitten's rough tongue touched his hand, "Well, you've got eight lives left, at that. As I see it, you should devote them all to catching mice—for me."

Wearily he threw himself down in one of the wide soft chairs that were his greatest luxury. But when the kitten cried softly, because it felt abandoned, he got up again. And taking the tiny thing softly into his arms, he went back to the chair.

The kitten snuggled up against his chest. The kitten yawned, in a languorous moment of peace after the storm. The doctor yawned, too.

* * *

When the maid who came mornings to tidy up entered the living room, they were still in the chair, sleeping—a man with a curious pallor on his still face and a mere scrap of a kitten with a front paw in splints and bandages.

The maid, being, by this time, immune to the oddity of physicians, tiptoed through the living room and out toward the kitchen. She made coffee and toast. She pushed the coffee pot to the back of the stove and ate the toast, herself.

It was ten o'clock, perhaps, when she tiptoed through the living room again to answer the buzz of the front door bell. The doctor was still sleeping; so was the kitten. She opened the door with her finger to her lips.

A girl stood there. A pretty, rather plump girl in a fur coat. A girl with trembling lips and dark circles under her eyes.

"I want to see Ned," the girl began. "The doctor," she corrected primly.

The maid recognized the girl. She'd dusted the frame around her picture every day for months. But she was a glum maid; she didn't smile.

"The doctor's asleep," she said. "Can I take a message?"

The girl spoke with a rush. "I'm not a patient," she said. "I am . . . I was a friend of the doctor's. He . . . he dropped something yesterday in my house. I . . . I found it on the floor after he'd gone. It's something valuable. I wanted to return it to him."

The maid relaxed. She almost achieved a pleasant expression.

"You can wait," she said. "I guess. He . . ." a jerk of her hand indicated a figure in a great chair—a figure seen on a slant through an inner doorway, "he can't sleep *much* longer!"

The girl stepped into the apartment and closed the front door after her. She wasn't a stranger to the place; she'd been there before. She went straight through the inner doorway into the living room. And paused before the miracle of that room.

The miracle of a table littered with cotton and bandages and medicine droppers and teaspoons and saucers of clotting milk and—calm among the litter—a girl's portrait in a frame of white jade.

The miracle of a chair with an exhausted man sprawled in it. A man with a smudge of dust on one cheek and a slight film of beard such as most men have before shaving time and his collar wrenched open at the throat and threads of lint from torn bandages clinging to his trousers.

Of a man sleeping dreamlessly with a wee morsel of a black kitten curled up on his chest. *Almost* curled, for one paw was held out stiffly in splints.

The man didn't waken as Evie crossed the room on light, incredulous feet. But the black kitten's eyes came suddenly open. And its pink mouth came open, too, in a yawn. The yawn turned into a tiny yap of pain as the kitten tried to stretch. Stretching wouldn't be easy for quite a few days, yet!

Evie looked at the kitten. She looked at the sleeping man. And then all at

once her round little face was glorified, and her eyes were as tender as Mary's eyes must have been on the very first Christmas Day of all.

Very quietly she opened the purse that she carried. It was a frivolous blue purse with a tassel. She took something from it—something that glimmered like the kind of a tear that grows out of extreme happiness. She slipped that something upon the third finger of her left hand. And then she sat down in a chair, still very quietly, to wait.

She was so quiet, in fact, that the small kitten yawned again and went back to sleep.

* * * * *

"Small Things," by Margaret E. Sangster, Jr., published in Sangster's The Littlest Orphan and Other Christmas Stories, *Round Table Press, New York, 1928. If anyone can provide knowledge of the origin and first publication source of this old story, please relay this information to Joe Wheeler (P.O. Box 1246, Conifer, CO 80433). Margaret E. Sangster, Jr. (1894–1981), author of "The Littlest Orphan," "Little Lonely Tree," and "With a Star on Top," was one of the most beloved inspirational writers in America early in the twentieth century. Now, after teetering on the brink of oblivion for fifty years, she is coming back. And we are all so much the richer for it!*

Back to the Heartland

-P. J. Platz-

Katherine had returned for but one reason—to sell the old place. After all, Chicago was her home now.

Or was it?

* * *

Katherine eased the car's stubby nose to within a foot of the picket fence, then turned off the key and stared dully through the dusty windshield at the ramshackle frame house.

It looks dead, she thought, hating the sight of the overgrown lawn, the crumbling steps, the unchecked creeper vines smothering the porch railing. In another week or so, the vine's fat shiny leaves would unfurl to the June sun, and you wouldn't be able to see the porch at all.

She was squeezing the steering wheel unconsciously, opening and closing her hands in the mindless motions of someone holding on, then letting go.

She rolled the window all the way down and leaned back against the headrest, closing her eyes. No need to hurry in. She'd waited five years to do what she would do this summer. A few more minutes wouldn't make much difference.

Her ears remembered the sounds she thought she'd forgotten—a laboring tractor in a nearby field; the lazy chirp of a drowsing sparrow; the steady, monotonous hum of flies finding the ideal place to sun on the hot metal of the car. *Nebraska,* she thought—*land of unending, boring quiet.* She missed Chicago already.

The guilt was still with her, gnawing at her, and after all this time, she'd begun to think it would never leave. She should have visited more often. Maybe she should never have moved away. Maybe her parents wouldn't have been in that particular car on that particular rain-slicked road at that particular time, if only she had been here.

And that was what it all boiled down to, that was really the reason she hadn't come back to sell the farm before now—because here she had to face the guilt. It stared out at her from every vacant window, reminding her that she had no right to be here now, after they were gone. They had been her only link to this place, and without them, she didn't belong here anymore. Lately she'd begun to wonder if she belonged anywhere.

She compressed her lips into a thin line and climbed from the car, then reached in for a bag of groceries. She had stopped for supplies at Potter's store on her way through town, and the locals had greeted her like the prodigal child come to her senses at last, come home to stay. None of her explanations about being here to fix up the farm to sell were even considered seriously.

Old Mrs. Potter praised the Lord for providing a teaching vacancy at the elementary school, just when Katherine Rhodes had decided to come home, and refused to listen to Katherine's insistence that she had no intention of giving up her position at Chicago Lakeside Elementary School.

She'd left the store after ten minutes, her head throbbing from beating it against the stone wall of their stubborn certainty that they knew her future far better than she did.

What *was* it about these people? she asked herself angrily, kicking open the sagging gate, turning sideways to squeeze through the narrow opening with the grocery bag perched on her hip. They never let go. Ever. Born here, raised here, died here. As if there were no other place on earth that was worth living in but this dusty little town, squatting in the middle of the Midwestern plains like a piece of forgotten litter.

She dropped her bag on the worn boards of the front porch and sighed, fitting the old brass key carefully into the lock. The heavy deadbolt slid back with surprising smoothness. After five years of nonuse, the mechanism should have been rusted and stubborn. She was struck by the fanciful, disturbing thought that the old house wanted to make it as easy as possible for her to get in.

She leaned back against the door frame and stared up the long, narrow stairway. It had been five years since she'd set foot on those stairs. Five years since that horrid double funeral.

"Well, here I am at last," she said aloud, then shivered, almost afraid the house would answer.

She shook off the unpleasant sensation with an angry jerk of her head and started through the late-afternoon gloom of the living room. She stopped halfway across the silent room and felt the tiny hairs on the back of her neck prickle.

"Silly," she said under her breath. "Stupid."

Yet, the certainty persisted that she was not alone in the house—perhaps not alone in this room. With a sense that defied understanding, she knew, absolutely *knew*, that there was another presence filling the dead, silent air around her.

She moved only her eyes in short, wary jerks, afraid to move even her head, afraid to breathe. The room was empty, as far as the limited range of her vision could discern. The yellowing curtains hung still in the breathlessness of the confined space. The ancient grandfather clock stood silent there in the corner. Her father's old recliner squatted in a layer of dust.

But her mother's chair—where was her mother's chair? The straight-backed Victorian horror—where was that? And then she remembered. The chair was behind her, tucked into the corner, in the one spot she couldn't see. And it wasn't empty. She could feel that without even turning around to look.

"Please, God," she whispered, trying to swallow the bitter lump that had to be her heart, pounding its way up to her throat. She tightened her grip on the grocery bag, then spun to face the chair.

In the space of her single, shrill scream, large yellow eyes blinked at her in languid indifference. Then the cat jumped gracefully from the chair and began lapping up the milk that had spilled when the groceries had tumbled from Katherine's grasp to crash on the floor.

She stood paralyzed, numbed by fear, shock, and then foolish relief. She was thinking that nothing in her life would ever frighten her so much again when the front door crashed against the wall, and she squeezed her eyes shut and screamed a second time.

A few pounding thumps shook the floor, then a voice bellowed, "Hey! What's going on here?"

Her eyelids fluttered, then fixed on a vague, blurry shape that congealed rapidly into the form of a large, powerful man. He took one look at her face, then guided her carefully to the couch.

"You sit down a minute before you fall down. I'll be right back," he said gruffly.

She sat perfectly, rigidly still on the dusty old couch, looking across the room to where an angular orange tabby still lapped at the spilled milk. *It's deaf,* she thought senselessly, making an automatic connection between her own screams and the cat's complete lack of response. *It has to be. Stone-cold deaf.*

As if sensing her thoughts, cold yellow eyes glanced up from the delicate work of the dainty pink tongue, then half-closed in concentration on the business at hand. Sharp shoulder blades jutted up in two angular points from the cat's crouch, marking extreme age and leanness. Battered, tipless ears tilted back along the bony head toward hollowed hips and a long, thick tail.

"Who in the world are you?" she asked the cat, then stiffened at the sudden squeal of the kitchen faucet.

"Well . . . ," the man had to duck to avoid the low header on the kitchen doorway. "Well," he said again, drawing closer to the couch, holding out a glass of water in one huge hand. "Feeling better?"

Katherine took the glass and sipped, grimacing at the heavy iron taste. "I'm fine, thanks. I was just startled, that's all."

He stood awkwardly in front of her, as if carrying the water glass had been the only possible thing he could think of to keep his body occupied. She handed the glass back with a grateful smile, and he took it quickly.

"Where did you come from?" she asked him.

"Oh." His face colored under the deep brown of a tan that had been building since spring plowing began. "Sorry about busting in like that. Tractor broke right next to your east fence, so I was close enough when I heard you scream. What happened? Charlie scare you?"

"Charlie?"

He jerked his head toward the cat, now totally occupied with the serious task of washing one front paw.

"Oh. So that's his name." She frowned and straightened a little, the seeds of anger beginning to smolder. "Yes," she said sharply, pushing a wayward dark curl from her eyes. "He certainly did. And I'd like to know what your cat is doing in my house."

"*My* cat? What makes you think he's *my* cat?"

"Well, you know him."

"Oh. That." His face lifted with the white slash of a slow grin. "Everybody knows Charlie. He's almost a legend around here. And if he's anybody's cat, he's yours. Provided that you're Katherine Rhodes, of course."

"How did you know who I was?"

"Are you kidding?" His whole face lifted with his smile. "In this town? About three minutes after you called Joe at Rural Electric to have the power turned on, everyone knew Katy Rhodes was coming home."

She breathed an exasperated sigh. "Well, I am Katherine Rhodes," she said stiffly, "but that creature is certainly not my cat. I don't even like cats, and I've never seen this one before in my life."

He kicked idly with one booted foot, watching it scrape back and forth across the dust on the floor. "He was your mother's cat," he said slowly, the grin fading. "A wild old tom, really. Never would tolerate anyone but your mom. She found him in the woods with a broken leg. Wildest, meanest, scruffiest thunderball of fur you ever saw. He scratched her up good, but she splinted the leg and brought

him around eventually. Still, she was the only human ever to touch him. He never trusted anybody else." He looked over at the cat and smiled, shaking his head. "He's not afraid of anything or anybody, that old tom. But watch this."

He walked softly over to where the cat suddenly stopped licking his paw, pink tongue still protruding slightly, eyes fixed on the approaching man. When the large human crouched next to him, the cat only stiffened slightly. When a hand was extended toward him, the angular beast straightened and managed a backward step with dignity. But when the hand reached too close, the cat was gone in a thrusting bound too fast for Katherine's eyes to follow.

The man straightened and grinned. "See what I mean? A few folks tried to catch him when your folks died, but there was no catching Charlie. This was his home and where he meant to stay. We knew he was getting into the house, but we never could find out how. Besides, he doesn't seem to bother much. He hunts at night and comes in to sleep during the day. He just lives here."

"I never knew Mom had a cat," she said a little resentfully.

"You'd have to live here to know that. He wasn't around much when he was younger."

And neither was I, Katherine thought, her heart constricting with guilt once again. *But I should have been. She was my mother, and I loved her, and I'm not even sure she knew that.*

She blinked hard once, then looked up into eyes of such a light blue that they looked almost transparent. "I don't know you, do I?"

"Sorry," he said sheepishly. "I'm Tom Harris. Your neighbor."

She let that one slide. He'd learn soon enough that she had no intention of becoming anyone's neighbor in this forsaken backwater town.

"Walter Harris was my uncle. I moved in from out East when he left me the farm . . . oh, must be seven years now."

Her nod was like a check mark. Walter Harris had died. Another thing she hadn't known, and Walter had been her father's best friend.

"I'm real sorry about your folks, by the way. I hadn't been here long before the accident, but I sure miss having them around."

Her smile was automatic, almost imperceptible. It had been five years, and people were still offering sympathy. "It was a long time ago," she mumbled, wondering why all of a sudden it didn't seem that way.

"Well, I didn't know you at all then, so I didn't want to bother you at the funeral, but I sure liked your folks. A man couldn't ask for better neighbors."

Why was he talking about this as if it had just happened? Why didn't he just shut up and get back to his stupid tractor and his stupid fields and . . .

"Well, I'll be going now. If I can give you a hand getting settled in, I'd be proud to help. Just call."

"Actually, I'm not going to be settling in, Mr. Harris."

"Tom."

"I'm just here long enough to spruce up the place to sell, then I'll be going home again."

"Home?" He frowned. "But I thought . . ."

"No," she broke in firmly. "I live in Chicago. I'll be going back just as soon as possible."

He nodded slowly, a little line appearing between his brows. "I see. Well, now, that's too bad. I was looking forward to having a Rhodes for a neighbor again. And that was even before I got a look at you."

Katherine smiled at the reserved, almost indiscernible compliment.

"At least let me take you out to dinner sometime before you leave. Who knows? Maybe I can talk you out of going back to Chicago."

She laughed out loud. "My parents would have told you that that's a losing battle."

He shrugged easily, then grinned. "So's farming," he said, then walked for the door.

Katherine caught herself peeking around corners that entire first evening, looking for that low-down sneaky cat—never quite sure she was alone in the house. "Oh, Chicago," she whispered as she eased into bed that night, weary from the hours she'd spent scrubbing the kitchen, wishing she were in her own bed in her own little, neat suburban house where everything was too new and tidy to hide decades of memories in every dark corner.

She closed her eyes and tried to force sleep, but the memories came instead.

Daguerreotype images of her father, with his perpetual lazy smile and his eyes screwed permanently into a squint. Brilliant flashes of her mother, the way she had looked when the peas first came in or when an oriole landed on the old stump in the backyard—aging eyes wide with the wonder of a child seeing something marvelous for the very first time.

"You'll come back, of course," her mother had said, uncertainty filling the clear blue eyes. "Oh, I know you don't think so. Not now, anyway. But blood runs deep, no matter how different we seem. You're still a Rhodes, Katy. Still your mother's daughter, and this is your place, just like it's been mine and your daddy's and his daddy's before him."

But her mother had known, had understood better than anyone else had, that Katherine's drummer pounded a more vibrant, distant beat; that something outside the Rhodeses' legacy of land and family and home pulled at her; and that she might never come back.

She rolled her face into the pillow and pressed deep into it, concentrating fiercely on the night sounds slipping through the open window. Crickets and frogs and the mournful hoot of a lonely owl, and then the sharp, shattering screech of something small, protesting death with its last breath. *The cat,* she thought. *The nightly hunt must have been successful.*

As if in confirmation, an eerie, elongated yowl pierced the night, and Katherine finally fell asleep wondering how the old bones could manage the physical rigors of stalk and kill.

Tom was there before she'd finished her morning coffee, tapping hesitantly at the back door with that curious respect farmers have for city people who sleep past first light.

"Good morning," he said shyly, bobbing his head until a bright shaft of blond spilled over his forehead. "Is it too early to talk business?"

She pushed open the sagging screen door and drew her housecoat more closely around her. "Business?" she echoed, waving him to the kitchen table, automatically filling another cup.

He nodded his thanks as he sat down. "I'd like to buy the farm," he said, "if you're bound and determined to sell, that is."

Katherine felt his eyes on her as she hesitated, startled by the unexpected offer.

"You sure you want to sell?" he asked softly.

She got up from her chair to refill her cup. "You just took me by surprise, that's all. I didn't know it would be this easy."

She eased back into her chair and studied the face opposite her. He had that same distance-gazing look in his eyes her father had had—and that same quiet expression of total contentment. But there was something else there—something lively and faintly amused, like a secret kept hidden from the rest of the world.

"Something about you doesn't look like a farmer," she said suddenly.

"And there's something about you that does," he replied softly.

A frown sharpened her features. "I'll have an appraisal done as soon as possible. It might take a week or so."

"That's fine by me. I'm in no hurry. Where's Charlie, by the way?"

"Charlie? Oh. The cat. I have no idea. Haven't seen him."

"Did you look in your mother's chair?"

She hustled him out after that, partly because she was uncomfortable still in her housecoat, partly because she resented his knowing that the stupid cat would be sleeping in her mother's chair.

She stood stiffly in front of the faded Victorian, staring down at the scruffy yellow bundle of jutting bones and matted fur. She stifled the impulse to reach out and fling the cat from the faded rose cushion where her mother used to sit.

"I wish you'd come home more often, Katherine." Her mother's voice seemed to fill the silent house. "We don't ever have enough time together."

Katherine squeezed her eyes shut tight and clenched her fists. She'd always meant to come more often, but she'd been so busy. Busy, busy, busy—with what? Things she couldn't even remember anymore.

"It never used to be like this," her father had complained once. "Families scattered hundreds of miles apart, not knowing each other at all. In the old days, the family stayed close, close enough for Sunday dinners together. That's what it was like when I was a boy. Home meant something then."

Katherine opened dry eyes and stared at the chair, her father's voice still echoing in her head.

Later that afternoon, Katherine waved Tom over from the field next door to share a glass of lemonade.

"Thanks," he said, accepting the glass and draining it immediately.

"You startled me there for a minute," he smiled, wiping perspiration from his brow with a bright red bandanna. "You looked just like your mom, beating on that old rug."

"I don't look at all like my mother," Katherine said quietly, remembering the tall, elegant figure so unlike her own petite sturdiness.

"Oh, your hair is darker and you're not as tall, but you move the same. And there's something in the eyes . . ." He stared at her with a little half-smile, as if he saw something in her face she didn't know was there. "I'd say there was a lot of your mother in you."

But there wasn't. Nothing of that deep contentment, that abiding serenity that always overshadowed the lines of age and hardship that had traced a careless map across her mother's gentle face. If she reminded Tom of her mother, it was only because her mother's image still lingered here, right where it belonged.

"Nobody ever said that before," she said quietly. "And you wouldn't either, if you'd ever seen us together. Even my dad used to say we clashed like two cymbals, we were so different."

"Maybe he was too close to both of you to see it."

"No." Katherine's smile was a little sad. "I'm afraid he was right. In a way, I wish I had been more like her—more like both of them. The child they always wanted."

"Weren't you?"

She laughed harshly. "My goodness, no. If I had been, I would have stayed right here in this town, taught at the school, married a farmer, and spent the rest of my life raising babies and homegrown peas."

Tom's smile was patronizing, but gently so. "Sounds pretty awful," he teased.

"OK," she conceded reluctantly. "Not a bad scenario for some, but it wasn't exactly what I had in mind. Mom and Dad could never get used to that. Believe it or not, they spent most of their time dreaming up ways to lure me back here, away from sinful Chicago."

She sighed and looked out over the cornfields that seemed to stretch forever, with infant green plants marching in orderly rows all the way to the horizon. "Sometimes I think they're still working on me," she mused, then shook her head quickly and blushed.

A blur of yellow shot through the edge of her peripheral vision as the cat sped around the corner of the house. He knew exactly where he was going and exactly how to get there. Even he belonged here more than she did.

"That cat gives me the creeps," she said suddenly, almost bitterly. "Why on earth does he stay here?"

Tom shrugged, a nonchalant gesture that contrasted sharply with the intensity of his gaze. "This is his home," he said simply. "Although the kids in town have glorified him a bit. They claim he's waiting for his mistress to return."

Katherine snorted and hefted the old wire carpet beater to an attack position.

Tom stopped her with a gentle touch on her arm. "I was serious, you know— about the dinner invitation. Tonight?"

She hesitated for a moment, reluctant to involve herself with any of the locals, then scoffed at her own misgivings. The man was just inviting her to dinner, after all. Not to the altar.

"OK." She smiled. "I'd like that."

He nodded and grinned. "I'll be by at seven. Thanks for the lemonade."

He is a nice man, Katherine thought later, dusting her way up the wooden banister that climbed the stairs. *A very nice man.* And he belonged here too, just as her mother and her father and their cat did. She was the only outsider. Why couldn't anyone else see that? Why hadn't her parents seen that? Why had they tortured themselves and her, trying to make her fit into the mold she'd been fighting so long? And why now, when she was out of range of their pleading eyes and their gentle persuasions, did she feel the pull more than ever?

I'm not like you, Mom. She heard the old litany in her memory. *I'm not a bit like you.*

She dropped the dust rag at the top of the stairs and went into her bedroom to lie on the faded quilt, closing her eyes against the afternoon sun shining through the window.

She didn't notice the sudden weight at the foot of the bed right away. It was only when it began to pace upward, toward her head, that she opened her eyes and saw the cat. It moved slowly, cautiously, placing one foot delicately forward, then hesitating, watching her warily for any sudden, threatening moves before putting his weight down fully. Yellow eyes gleamed in the afternoon sun, pupils so constricted in the light that she could barely see the slits of black focused so intently on her face.

"Miserable cat," she grumbled, not caring if she frightened him away, holding out one hand as if to block his progress.

Charlie's head shot up and back at the sudden motion of the hand, then he stretched his neck forward carefully, little nostrils flickering to catch the scent of the fingers that seemed to be reaching for him. When the cold, wet of his nose finally made contact with her hand, he closed his eyes and made a strange noise deep in his throat, then butted under her hand with tail straight up and back arched, satisfied now that this was the scent he had been looking for, this was the hand he had been waiting for, all these years.

He paced back and forth under her hand while Katherine watched wide-eyed, obediently stroking the scruffy fur while her mind repeated all the things she had been told about Charlie. *He was your mother's cat. . . . Never would tolerate anyone but your mom. . . . He never trusted anybody else. . . . He's waiting for his mistress to return. . . .*

Charlie curled into a ball at her side, resting his head on his front paws, the rumble of his purring vibrating against her ribs, and Katherine felt the gentle tug of an invisible line that still bound her to her mother, her father, this place.

"Charlie," she whispered, and the cat lifted his head to blink languidly at her. "Charlie, you stupid old cat. You think I'm Mom, don't you? Well, you're wrong. You know I'm not a bit like she was."

For some reason, the cat reminded her of Mrs. Potter—staring at her, blinking calmly, as if to say that he knew perfectly well who she was, even if she didn't.

And something inside her jolted into sudden, perfect alignment with everything else, and she knew that the cat was right.

"I am my parents' child," she whispered, letting the tears run freely at last because her parents would never know that. Then again, perhaps they always had.

She had the preposterous, uncanny notion that this was the last persuader—the last lure to bring her home, to show her where she belonged—and that her parents had left old Charlie behind just to keep the door open.

"Nonsense," she muttered, letting her head fall back on the pillow, stroking the matted fur absently with one hand. "That's just plain nonsense."

She wondered if her eyes would be all puffy and red for her dinner with Tom tonight. And she wondered if he would mind very much if she didn't sell him the farm. Somehow, she didn't think so.

She fell asleep in the middle of the afternoon, on a sun-splashed bed, her hand resting on Charlie's back.

The old yellow tom raised his head slowly, annoyed that the stroking had stopped. Then he sighed heavily and dropped his chin back to his paws. His mistress would wake up eventually, and then she would pat him again. All he had to do was wait, and Charlie was very good at waiting.

* * * * *

"Back to the Heartland," by P. J. Platz. Reprinted by permission of Tracy and Patricia Lambreche. P. J. Platz is a successful mother/daughter writing team who live in Chicago City, Minnesota. They are prolific writers of short stories, novels, and movie scripts, and their work is carried by contemporary women's and family magazines.

The Undoing of Morning Glory Adolphus

-N. Margaret Campbell-

Adolphus was used to ruling supreme over the household. Then came that insufferable upstart, Silver Paws, who replaced him. So how might the dethroned monarch regain his kingdom?

* * *

Morning Glory Adolphus is our oldest and most sedate cat. He has his own hunting preserve in a wooded ravine at the back of our house, and woe to the cat or dog who invades it. In his early youth he won an enviable reputation as a hunter of big game, and he has his own method of securing due recognition for his exploits. Whenever he captures a rabbit, a squirrel, a water rat, or a snake, he hunts until he finds his mistress and lays the tribute proudly at her feet. This determination to be cited for bravery and prowess becomes a trifle embarrassing at times, especially when he drags a five-foot snake into the music room and lets it wriggle on the rug to the horror and confusion of guests. But whatever the hazards, Adolphus is not to be thwarted of due publicity for his skill. If he were a man, he would be accompanied on all of his hunting trips by a press agent and would have luncheon with the editors of all the sporting journals upon his return. As it is, without even a correspondence course in advertising, Adolphus manages quite well.

For the study of majestic dignity, tinged on occasion with lofty disdain, interpreters of muscular expression would do well to seek out Adolphus. He walks the highway without haste or concern for his personal survival in the midst of tooting automobiles and charging dogs. When a strange dog appears and mistakes Adolphus for an ordinary cat who may be chased for the sport of the thing, it is the custom of Adolphus to slow his pace somewhat and stretch out in the path of the oncoming enemy, assuming the pose and the expression of the sphinx. He is the carven image of repose and perfect muscular control. Only his slumberous amber eyes burn unblinkingly, never leaving the enraged countenance of his enemy, who bears down upon him with exposed fangs and hackles erect. When the assault is too ferocious to be in good taste even among dogs, accompanied by hysterical yapping and snapping, Adolphus has been known to yawn in the face of his assailant, quite deliberately and very politely, as a gentleman of good breeding might when bored by an excessive display of emotion. Usually the dog mysteriously halts within a foot or

so of those calm yellow eyes and describes a semicircle within range of those twin fires, filling the air with defiant taunts that gradually die away to foolish whimpering as he begins an undignified withdrawal, while Adolphus winks solemnly and stares past his cowering foe into a mysterious space undesecrated by blustering dogs.

A few dogs there have been who have failed to halt at the hypnotic command of those yellow eyes. Then there came a lightninglike flash of fur through the air, and Adolphus landed neatly on his victim's neck, his great claws beginning to rip with businesslike precision through the soft ears and forehead of the terrified dog. Perhaps the rumor of these encounters spread among the canine population of our neighborhood, for it is never counted against the reputation of any dog as a fighter if he makes a wide detour of the regions frequented by Adolphus.

For years the rule of Adolphus among the cats of his own household has been undisputed. Then came Silver Paws, a handsome young rogue whose satiny coat was beautiful with broken silver and blue lights. There was no question about it, Silver Paws had a way with the ladies. While Adolphus still looked upon him as a frolicsome kitten whose sense of humor was unbalanced by a proper sense of dignity, Silver Paws artfully won all hearts and easily became the center of attraction wherever he appeared. It was plainly disgusting to Adolphus to see the way the conceited young thing arched his back expectantly whenever a human hand came near enough to caress him.

If Adolphus had had the small mind of a punster, he might have observed, after the cynical manner of others who have lost their place in the public affections to an unworthy rival, that the glory was passing out of his name. But he was never one to surrender without a struggle. He went to his nightly hunt with cold murder in his heart and a high resolve to force the spotlight back upon himself. Daily he laid at the feet of his mistress older and wilier rabbits, fiercer-eyed rats, and longer snakes. All to no purpose. He even played the heroic role of the deliverer when his hated rival was treed by the grocer's dog. He simply walked calmly up to the tree where the dog was dancing wildly under the limb where the trembling Silver Paws clung, and the dog suddenly remembered that he really ought to catch up to the grocer's wagon and that it wasn't much fun to bark at a silly kitten anyway! When the frightened Silver Paws slid down the tree, Adolphus walked up to him with the self-righteous air of a benevolent gentleman who has rescued a lost soul not because the soul deserved it, but because he himself was made that way. This magnanimous act gave Adolphus a momentary advantage over his rival, but the fickle attentions of the household were soon centered upon the handsome young charmer again. Then Adolphus took to sitting about the house, gazing solemnly past the spot where Silver Paws was receiving the choicest bits of meat with many endearing words, and smoothed his whiskers with a reflective paw.

It was about this time that Silver Paws, to the consternation of the household, disappeared. A search was instituted in the neighborhood, but he was gone without a trace, just as though there had been some witchery abroad and he had been whisked away on a magic broom. Mournfully we gathered up the playthings he had left scattered over the house—a bit of fur on a string, a bright-colored ball, some dried beans that rattled in the pod when batted about by a velvet paw—and of these remembrances we made a heap in his favorite rocking chair. "He'll want them if he ever comes back," we said.

A remarkable change had come over Morning Glory Adolphus. We had long honored him as a crafty hunter and a first-rate fighting man, but we had judged him to be somewhat lacking in sentiment, a trifle indifferent and unresponsive, as was natural enough in one who had achieved no small amount of fame. What was our astonishment to find that he had become, overnight, warmly demonstrative in his affections and sympathetically desirous of turning our thoughts from useless brooding over the lost one. It was really touching to see the way he followed us about the house, sitting at our feet to sing with rapturous abandon wherever we happened to pause. Forgotten were the joys of the chase, the pleasant pastime of disciplining unmannerly dogs. For three whole days he gave himself up wholly to the business of lovemaking. If we attempted to ignore him, he threw himself at our feet and lay on his back at our mercy, as one who would say that he bared his faithful heart that we might kill him if we could not love him. He walked about the house with the proudly possessive air of a haughty ruler who has returned to his domains after an enforced absence, and he curled up blissfully on the cushions where his late rival had been accustomed to take his ease. Once we found him stretched contemptuously over the playthings that lay in a little heap in the rocking chair. It must have been a bumpy sort of bed, but Adolphus looked happy and comfortable.

Suspicion instantly seized upon his mistress. "Adolphus," she said sternly, "I believe you know what has become of our beautiful Silver Paws!" The accused rose stiffly to his full height, regarded her with the gravely innocent expression of an outraged deacon, and then, turning his back deliberately upon her, gave himself up again to the slumbers of the just.

But the suspicious of the household were not so easily allayed. "Adolphus is trying too hard to be good," they argued. "It is not natural. There must be something on his conscience!" For this was Adolphus's way of raising a smoke screen, as it were, to hide his evil deeds. They had observed this in the past. It was all very humiliating to a proud soul like Adolphus, and he showed his resentment by stalking out of the house and letting the screen door slam behind him after the manner of any offended male.

The household followed him from afar. He walked straight to the ravine, where he was accustomed to hunt, and stood peering intently down into it over the edge of a cliff, his ears pricked forward, every line of him expressing gloating satisfaction, from his agitated whiskers to the tip of his quivering tail. It was hard to believe that he was the same kindly creature who had been making affectionate advances to us a few hours before. As we drew near we could hear a faint crying, pleading and pitiful, and down among the bushes we discovered our lost Silver Paws, too weak from loss of food to stand, and rather battered from the rough treatment he had received from his jailer.

The moment that Adolphus saw us looking into the ravine he withdrew in disgust, for he knew that his game was up. With lofty scorn he watched us gather up his banished rival, revive him with warm milk, caress and comfort him. With what dire threats had Adolphus kept his captive down in the ravine, within sound of our voices, all the long hours while he wooed us at his leisure, and what spell had he cast over him that the hungry kitten had not dared to come at our call?

While we rejoiced and scolded, the grocer's dog was observed coming around the corner of the house. He had grown bold during those days of weakness when Adolphus had been courting the ladies. But one look into the amber eyes of Adolphus, and he was off with a shriek, for he could see that the fighter was once more master of his domain.

* * * * *

"The Undoing of Morning Glory Adolphus," by N. Margaret Campbell. Published June 1922 in St. Nicholas. *Text reprinted by permission of Joe Wheeler (P.O. Box 1246, Conifer, CO 80433). N. Margaret Campbell wrote for popular magazines during the early part of the twentieth century.*

Black Cats and Becky

Becky was so superstitious her roommates almost gave up on her. Superstitious especially about black cats.

So what could they do to change her mind?

* * *

Becky's forever-dancing gray eyes were somber as she gave her decision to her two roommates. Under her soft Louisiana drawl was a firmness that made Wanda and Janice certain she could not be dissuaded from her refusal to sing that night at Raneleigh Seminary's big competitive concert.

"But Becky!" wailed Janice. "Do you realize that our Golds won't stand the remotest chance to defeat the Maroons if you turn us down now? We've no singer who can hold a candle to you! And think how ridiculous you'd seem to the whole school just because of some silly superstitions!"

Becky's lips tightened. "So you all think it's silly that a black cat just sprang out at me on the campus? And it's silly that I've dreamed three nights in a row of muddy water? Why, that's the surest sign of trouble there is!"

Plump little Wanda snatched off her glasses and began wiping them vigorously on the hem of her skirt, as she invariably did when nervous or desperate. Her glasses were always bent out of shape.

"You're afraid, Becky Kenyon," she snapped peremptorily. "You've never sung in front of so many people before, and it's got you down."

"Afraid?" Becky echoed in dismay, not seeing through her roommate's age-old, obvious wile. "Why, I'd revel in the opportunity to sing those wonderful songs, but . . ." She shrugged dismally. "I reckon it's too late, for you should never do an important thing on a Friday, anyhow—of all days. When I tripped and fell over the steps last Monday after my rehearsal with Miss Dale, that should have warned me in the first place. To fall on Monday, you know. All this week has been a constant warning, sure enough. Why, only last night," her voice dropped to almost a whisper, "I saw the new moon through the trees out yonder."

Wanda leaped up from her desk impatiently. "Fiddlesticks. You're hopeless, Becky—hopeless and handicapped! How do you suppose you'll ever mount the musical ladder, hampered as you are by these idiotic superstitions? Why, I should think your father would have been more careful than to let you pick up such ideas."

She stopped short, warned by the look in Becky's eyes at the reference to her father whom the southern girl idolized—the father who was all the world to her, since she was motherless.

"I'm sorry, Becky dear," Wanda muttered, and began rubbing her spectacles again.

Janice spoke hastily to cover up the blunder. She was older than Wanda and less awkward.

"After all, it's hard for us to understand the strange things you believe, Becky. I'm afraid we Golds are so earnest about swamping the Maroons tonight that we aren't being sympathetic. Don't you see, though, that with your glorious voice there would be no doubt of our team's victory? Oh, you must sing—even if you refuse to do it again all year, Becky!"

"That blond beauty of hers would win the judges' vote even if they weren't listening to the warbling," Wanda grinned, ever the bungler.

Janice frowned; her look labeled Wanda the proverbial bull in the china shop. Becky deliberately made no comment, but went toward the door.

"I'm going to run downstairs to the post office. The morning's mail ought to be in."

At the threshold she hesitated and wheeled about.

"I'm sorry to be such a poor sport, and I admit many such warnings have been false. But there is one I'll always heed, and that . . ." she faltered, ". . . that is what just happened outside."

Wanda snorted. "The old black mouser?"

"I've a very special fear of them," Becky said with quiet firmness. "You see,

when I was a baby, Nellie—the nurse who was caring for me— found a black cat in my carriage cuddled against my throat. Sure enough, the very next day my mother . . ." She shuddered, then went on rapidly. "The next time, our tenant farmer's house burned down. A black cat had run across Nellie's path that morning."

"I suppose both things would never have happened unless the poor cats had been handy on the scene?" Wanda scoffed. "How many times have you seen a black tabby when nothing at all happened?"

Becky turned to go. "Anyway, I'll not risk the concert tonight. My mind is made up. I'll tell Miss Sanford after I get our mail."

When she had gone, Janice dropped forlornly upon her bed. Wanda stared blankly out the window upon the Pennsylvania landscape, chartreuse with spring. For several minutes there was total silence.

It was Janice who spoke finally.

"You know, Wanda," she began earnestly, "at the opening of school Miss

Sanford told me that Becky's father had written to her, asking her to do everything she could to get Becky over the superstitions that Nellie had instilled in her. Naturally, with no playmates way out there on that remote sugar plantation, she was greatly influenced as a child by the woman. That is why Mr. Kenyon sent her up here to school, so she could be with other girls. And that is why Miss Sanford placed her with us, so . . ."

"Room number seven!" Wanda smiled wryly. "Becky chose it because 'odd numbers are lucky.' And no sooner had she arrived than she hung that horseshoe over the door, curved upward 'so the luck won't run out.' Becky does everything but carry the left hind foot of a rabbit, Jan! Why, she even sweetens her tea before putting in milk lest some day she be crossed in love!"

Janice sighed. "I know. But she is so lovely! You know there is hardly a girl at Raneleigh who isn't deeply grateful for some rare kindness Becky has shown her. Everybody adores her—a case where beauty is not skin-deep. Oh, Wanda, if only we could perform the miracle of curing her of her superstitions by tonight!"

Wanda grinned facetiously. "Might as well try to get the cook to serve us something besides baked beans and slaw for Wednesday's lunch! As hopeless. A girl who won't sing before breakfast, never puts her hat on a bed, wears her dresses wrong side out for luck on exam days, and is afraid to spill salt, can't be cured so magically!"

Janice nodded absently. "Becky's fear of cats is so inconsistent with her intense love for all animals," she mused. "She's forever bringing in strays. Remember, Wanda, the day she ran out bare-headed into that dreadful blizzard and rescued the puppy, then fed him for weeks with a nursing bottle?"

Wanda sniffed. "And he's kept me awake every Saturday morning since then with his yipping. If that's . . ."

But Janice cut her short with a sharp exclamation.

"Say! If Becky hasn't reached the head's office yet, I'll beat her to it! I'll wager Miss Sanford can persuade her to sing tonight if anybody can!"

She was out of room seven like a flash, leaving Wanda murmuring waggishly, "On to victory, lassie! And it's three cheers for the Golds—I hope."

* * *

The headmistress was not in her office. Disappointed, Janice hurried out to the secluded sun porch, thinking Miss Sanford might be there reading her mail.

The place was empty save for one girl, her face partly hidden among the pillows of a divan. It was Becky, worn out from much sobbing.

Instantly Janice was on her knees beside her roommate, her gentle voice comforting the forlorn girl. Without a word, Becky handed her a letter postmarked the day before from New York City. The handwriting was bold and masculine.

At her nod, Janice read its startling message:

> *Dear Little Girl:*
>
> *You wrote so enthusiastically and beautifully of the traditional musicale in which the school's rival divisions—the Golds and Maroons—are competing, that I scheduled my annual business trip to New York much earlier so I can hear you sing. My train should get me there a little before the Concert-of-My-Life.*
>
> *All the way up from home I pictured how you will look up there on the stage. Will you wear that Alice-blue gown? Also, if there is an encore will you sing for me the popular little song by that same name?*
>
> *Oh, Becky, I would not miss this treat for the whole world! I'm counting the very minutes. And remember: whether your side wins or not, you will be singing for the great joy of it and for your*   *Dad.*

Janice handed back the letter, her heart racing.

Becky's lips trembled. "The precious darling! For him to upset his business plans and make all that expensive trip, then have me fail him so miserably!"

Janice planted herself squarely in front of her roommate, and her manner was suddenly like Wanda's.

"You're not going to fail him!" she dictated fiercely. "You're not going to weep another tear, either! Have you forgotten what you told me about singers, Becky Kenyon? That emotional upsets are just the worst thing there is for them, that they send a poison through the system? So between now and eight o'clock you're to relax and practice deep breathing and humming beside an open window, and eat nothing but pineapple and . . ."

"You do believe a few things I say, apparently!" Becky ventured, slowly drying her tears.

"And you must take a long nap this afternoon so your voice will be rested," Janice rattled on.

Becky looked up wistfully. "Please, ma'am, Miss Maestro, may I take a little time out to go over my program once or twice if I do it in half-voice?"

The bell for classes drowned out Janice's elated reply. But all that day while she and Wanda plodded away in their classrooms, she felt an ecstatic glow, knowing that Becky was upstairs spending the time in the training she had prescribed. Already she was feeling generously sorry for the Maroons.

Becky was last on the program of vocal and instrumental music. And as she finished her first number, the audience sat thrilled and amazed that such rich, dramatic tones could be those of a seventeen-year-old girl.

Mistaking their silence, Becky's eyes sought her father's straight ahead of her down the aisle. His smile glowed as he gave a little encouraging nod. Then her happy assurance became that of the shepherd's sweetheart in "Florian's Song," by Godard—Wanda Milne's favorite. Her final selection she had made for Janice— that haunting Irish love song "Macushla." With her sweet, sensitive face uplifted in the closing pianissimo, she did not know a mist of sudden tears had come over the eyes of John Kenyon at the words "Death is a dream, and love is for aye."

When the thunderous, wild applause had demanded an encore and she had bowed gracefully in her dainty dress of blue tulle, obliging them with "Alice-blue Gown," Mr. Kenyon knew that his daughter's voice belonged no longer to him alone, but to the world. And when Miss Sanford rose at last to close the program, he did not hear a word she said; for the exquisite tones were still ringing in his ears.

But suddenly he was startled by the mention of Becky's name, and for the first time his eyes left his daughter to look at the tall, distinguished woman in velvet. What was she saying—"Maroons?" "Golds?"

Then in a flash, he knew. Standing with the Golds, cheering, were all the Maroons whom his Becky had vanquished but whose hearts she had stolen.

During the uproar Mr. Kenyon noticed the headmistress whispering excitedly to an austere-looking woman who was sitting with the trustees on one side of the platform. When the cheering was over, Miss Sanford came forward and spoke again.

"Now I have come to the great surprise of an evening already crowded with many happy surprises for you. It is my honor to have entertained this evening a lover of music, Mrs. Langdon Cavanaugh-Smith, of Philadelphia. Each year Mrs. Cavanaugh-Smith awards a scholarship of a year's study in Europe to that preparatory-school student or college student whom she considers sufficiently promising to merit such a course. It is for this reason that Mrs. Cavanaugh-Smith particularly requested me not to announce her presence before our program. She was afraid," Miss Sanford smiled with obvious pride, "there might be no one here who deserved such special training. But tonight she awards her scholarship to a Raneleigh girl, Miss Rebecca Anne Kenyon."

For a moment there was a breathless hush. Becky, standing inside the wings, turned white and pink by turns and leaned against the wall to support her sudden weakness. Out in the third row her father found himself trembling with over-whelming gladness. In a body the Golds and Maroons rose to their feet again. Then pandemonium broke loose while Becky was brought out of her retreat to the center of the stage. She felt as if the entire assemblage had swooped down upon her, con-gratulating, exclaiming, shaking hands, hugging her, laughing, besieging her with flowers.

Magically, then, everybody's attention turned to something far down the cen-ter aisle and the hubbub subsided a trifle. Becky stood on tiptoe to see over their heads.

Red-faced, perspiring, her crooked spectacles halfway down her nose, Wanda was pushing her way through the crowd. High above her head she balanced an enormous box tied with white tissue paper and a great red bow.

When at last she reached her roommate across the footlights, she grinned tri-umphantly and turned to face the crowd.

"This is a gift of luck and love from the Golds to their Becky!" she announced blushingly. Then she laid the box gingerly in the young singer's arms and fled, embarrassed.

A toss of the wrappings, a lifting of the bulging top, and the contents of the gift box lay exposed. A tiny black kitten! Around its neck a label had been tied with crimson ribbon; on it was printed: I BRING YOU GOOD LUCK.

For a second Becky's face was sober. Then it lit with a tender smile as she impetuously cuddled the soft little creature in her arms.

"You darling!" she whispered. "You're going to be called either 'Reform' or 'Lucky'! Daddy and Janice and Wanda'll know why, bless their hearts."

Peering from the wings, two conspirators knew the days of horseshoes and unlucky Fridays were numbered.

* * * * *

"Black Cats and Becky," by Dorothy Clayton Glenn. Published May 31, 1936, in The Girl's Companion. *Reprinted by permission of Joe Wheeler (P.O. Box 1246, Conifer, CO 80433) and Cook Communications Ministries, Colorado Springs, CO. Dorothy Clayton Glenn wrote for popular and inspirational magazines during the first half of the twentieth century.*

A Kitten by Post

-Estelle M. Hart-

Kitten Fluff thought it would be fun to play a trick on her mother. But oh, how sorry she was afterwards!

* * * * *

This is a story for very small children.

* * *

Kitten Fluff's birthplace was a big, round basket in the back room of the Rushtown Post Office. There she spent the first days of her life, with her two sisters, Kitten Gray and Kitten Spot. For the first week or two of their lives they were very quiet, contented kittens. All they wanted was to eat and sleep, and Mother Muff attended to their meals and kept the house—that is, the basket— very quiet while they slept. One day they found out two things: One was that the world wasn't bounded by the circumference of their basket; the other was that their legs were made to walk with. At first it was a great deal of trouble to make their legs go the way they wanted them to go, but after a few days' practice they found, to their great satisfaction, that their legs not only would go where they wanted them to but would go very fast, indeed. What fun they had when they found that out! How they scampered after each other and after Mother Muff if she chanced to go to the door to see what the weather was like! Mother Muff was very proud of her kittens. She said to herself that they were certainly the smartest family of kittens she had ever had; and, as they were the only ones she had ever had, I am quite sure she was right.

One day they went through the door into the post office. What a curious place it was! Kitten Gray and Kitten Fluff examined all the desks and chairs and nooks and corners, and got acquainted with Postmaster Jones and several of the clerks. But Kitten Spot, who was of a very quiet, uninvestigating turn of mind, was the one who found the mail bags. There they were—flat, empty things, thrown in a pile in a corner.

What a splendid place to lie down and take a nap! thought Kitten Spot; so she curled herself into a little ball on the leather bags.

Then Kitten Gray and Kitten Fluff thought that they were very tired also, and, following Kitten Spot's example, they cuddled down beside her and were fast asleep in a minute.

When Mother Muff walked in, a little later, she was shocked to see where her children were sleeping. She knew that mail bags are very precious things. She had heard of dreadful things that Uncle Sam had done to people who tampered with mail bags. She was almost sure she heard Uncle Sam's step outside. She picked up the kittens, one at a time, by the nice little handle at the back of their necks, and hurried with them to their good, safe basket. Then she gave them a long lecture about their conduct, which she was almost certain they would never forget. But whenever they went into the office, they always felt so sleepy when they got into the corner where the mail bags were, that they did forget, and were sure to get into a bunch and go to sleep.

Mother Muff was dreadfully worried, but after she learned that Postmaster Jones only laughed when he saw them there, she worried less. She thought that if that dreadful Uncle Sam should happen to come in perhaps Mr. Jones would plead for the kittens, and maybe Uncle Sam would excuse them, because they were so very young.

A Kitten by Post

One morning, when Kitten Spot was finishing her after breakfast nap, and Mother Muff was attending to Kitten Gray's bath, Kitten Fluff was enjoying a little waltz, with her tail for a partner. Before she knew it, she had waltzed through the open door into the post office and half across the room. Then she stopped short and with a great deal of dignity walked over to the mail bags. One of them was lying by itself, somewhat apart from the others, and was open a little. Kitten Fluff poked her nose inside. Then such a bright idea struck her! She would go into the bag and hide from Mother Muff. Mother Muff would think she was lost. How she would hunt for her, and how surprised she would be to find her in the depths of the bag! It was a very long way to the bottom of the bag, but Kitten Fluff pushed her way in and cuddled down very still, hiding her nose in her paws to smother a laugh. But before you could count ten she was asleep and dreaming of a great big rat she was going to catch when she grew up. All of a sudden, something hit her every so many raps. She sat straight up. She thought Mother Muff was boxing her ears. But it was something a great deal worse than that. There were dozens of letters (Mother Muff had told her what those funny paper things were) falling down on top of her. She was so frightened she couldn't stir. Then there was a terrible earthquake. Then the light was all shut out at the top of the bag, and she heard a little click. Oh, dear, it was so dark, and those dreadful letters kept pushing and crowding her so! She didn't want to hide from Mother Muff anymore, but called for her again and again. But, alas! The leather walls were very thick, and no sound reached Mother Muff's ears.

What a terrible time poor Kitten Fluff had! The bag was picked up and carried a long way, and thrown down again very hard. Kitten Fluff was pretty sure some of her bones must be broken. Then the air in the mail bag was very thin; she had a very bad headache and a dreadful palpitation of the heart. She was sure she was going to die. She wished she'd always been a good kitten, and she wished very, very much that she had never played hide-and-seek with her mother. Then came some strange rumbling noises all about her, which she could not understand at all. After a while she fell asleep, but she dreamed such a bad dream about a large dog that was running after her, that she was glad when she woke up.

After a long while (Kitten Fluff thought it must have been several years), the bag was moved again. She had another shaking, and lo, a wonderful thing happened! Somebody opened the end of the bag, and dumped her and all of the letters out upon a shelf in a very long, narrow room. For a minute she was so surprised she didn't know what to do, but the next instant she jumped down and rushed wildly across the floor to see if she still had use of her legs.

"Great Caesar!" said one of the men.

That wasn't Kitten Fluff's name, at all, but she was too much astonished to tell the man so.

A little man came up from the other end of the car—she heard the men call it a car afterward—and exclaimed, "Well, that's the most curious mail package I ever saw!"

Then the little man took her up by the nape of the neck, just as her mother always did. She liked that man very much.

"Well, I declare!" said he, "if this isn't one of those kittens that I saw up in the Rushtown Post Office last week. I can tell it by that odd white ring on its tail."

Kitten Fluff had never cared much for rings before, but she was very glad now that her tail was ornamented with one. She told all her troubles to the little man, in kitten language, and as he was something of a student in languages, he understood all she said. He said something to the big man about telegraphing ahead and having her sent back from Greatville. Kitten Fluff was a little worried at first, for she didn't suppose there was any way of going back except in a mail bag; but the little man looked so kind that she made up her mind to trust him, and went to sleep on his overcoat thrown over a chair.

Pretty soon the train stopped, and a man came to the car door with a light wooden box and a pan of milk.

Kitten Fluff had almost forgotten how hungry she was in her excitement. But she always lunched at ten o'clock, and now it was nearly noon, so that she really was very hungry indeed, and milk was her favorite food.

After she had lapped a great deal, the little man said, "No time to spare, Kit; the up-train is nearly due."

Then he put her in the wooden box and nailed some slats over one side. She didn't like it very much, but it was a vast improvement on the mail bag. There was some writing on the top of the box, which she couldn't see, but she caught sight of the big lettering: "WITH GREAT CARE." She wondered what that meant. She didn't have time to inquire, however, because another train came up just then by the side of theirs, and she was put into one of the cars on that train. She enjoyed the ride home very much, because she was near a window and could look out and enjoy the scenery.

It was late in the afternoon when the train reached Rushtown, and there at the station was the errand-boy, Mike, whom she knew quite well. He took the wooden box, with its big lettering, under his arm.

"Be jabers!" said he, "you're a foine traveler. I always said you was the loikeliest wan o' the lot."

What a time there was when Kitten Fluff reached the post office! The postmaster and all the clerks had some word of greeting for her, but there was no one else half so glad to see her as Mother Muff, and no one else whom Kitten Fluff was half so glad to see.

* * * * *

"A Kitten by Post," by Estelle M. Hart. Published August 1892 in St. Nicholas. *Text reprinted by permission of Joe Wheeler (P.O. Box 1246, Conifer, CO 80433). Estelle M. Hart wrote for turn-of-the-twentieth-century magazines.*

INKSPOT

-Louise Redfield Peattie-

It was only a dark blob of a little kitten—no bigger, it seemed, than an inkspot. Hence his name. But Inkspot was unwanted. In fact, he was condemned to death. Several times. And herein hangs the story.

* * *

From the beginning he wasn't wanted. Oh, of course his mother wanted him, and blind and ignorant as he was, he could feel, in the touch of her warm, eager little fingers, that Winnie wanted him. But Winnie's mother didn't, which was what really mattered. She didn't want any of them.

And they were very pretty kittens at that. All, that is, except the black one, who was certainly a scrawny, rusty, unattractive little worm, weakly wriggling under the stronger crowd of his greedy brothers and sisters. So that, as they grew older and their eyes opened to milky blue innocence, they all found welcoming homes among families in the neighborhood—all but the littlest black one. There was no one to want him. Winnie found him crying his faint, plaintive cry, in the woodpile, alone and hungry, and carried him in a passion of pity into the drawing room.

"It looks," said Uncle George, surveying the kitten where it stood unsteadily in the middle of the Aubusson carpet, "like a small, small blot of ink."

"And about as welcome," said his sister, with a vexed laugh. "Winnie dear, we simply can't keep him." And she rang for Isaiah, the old hired houseman.

Thus, in a burlap bag with a stone tied around the top, Inkspot went to his doom. Isaiah, carrying him toward the river, and shuffling along with the bag dangling forgotten from his old bony hand, never noticed when it grew a little lighter. Inkspot, standing in the dusty road, looked after him mildly, watched him hurl the loosely tied bag in a wide arc into the river, and then, as a cart came rumbling by, scuttled into the roadside weeds. When he emerged again, the old man was already some distance down the homeward road, and Inkspot, with an anxious mew, trotted after him.

The family was on the veranda when Inkspot, dusty and bedraggled, wobbled up the steps. He looked at them out of his innocent and hopeful blue eyes, and mewed. With a glad little cry Winnie ran to him and gathered him up in her arms.

"Put him down, Winnie," said her mother sharply. "George, however in the world . . ."

"It's very hard to kill a black cat," said Uncle George sagely.

But Winnie's mother was obdurate, and in the end it was Uncle George, himself, who carried the kitten downstairs, at arm's length, with a bottle in the other hand. There in the dungeon gloom of the basement he found a starch box, and thrust Inkspot under it. Next, he found a rag, and saturating it with the overpowering fluid from the bottle, he thrust that too under the box.

Uncle George never told how well or ill he slept that night. But he descended to the basement before breakfast. The starch box stood mutely in the middle of the floor, and he grimly took it up. Gladly crying, Inkspot dashed out and wreathed himself in happy gratitude about Uncle George's ankle.

No one heard Uncle George gasp, as he mopped his brow with his silk handkerchief. Inkspot, hungry and light-hearted, bounded up the cellar stairs, and Uncle George followed, too bewildered to look twice at the starch box, where it lay overturned, showing the little knot hole that had brought life all night to Inkspot's unhappy pink nose.

"I told you it couldn't be done," said Uncle George at breakfast, with an air of vindication. "Not a cat as black as that."

Winnie's tears and entreaties broke down her mother's determination. Inkspot, reprieved, was taken into the family. It was an interlude so perfect as to constitute a cat heaven. By the glowing hearth in the drawing room there was a place for Inkspot now, where he might lie with paws softly folded under him, purring like a boiling kettle and staring at the flames with eyes holding a mystery that since time's beginning has awed mankind.

As the halcyon days passed, Inkspot's spindly legs grew stronger, his heart gayer. He took to frisking in the middle of the Aubusson carpet, chasing his tail in that delirium of fluid grace so fascinating for clumsy humans to watch. And Winnie on the hearth rug would clap her hands and squeal in delight. Her mother, in the grown-ups' Olympus of proper chairs and tables, talked with a guest above the heads of the two young things.

"Old Isaiah is getting much too cranky anyway," Mother was saying, "and this new butler, my dear, is a marvel! English, and with the most perfect manner. He's been trained since boyhood, it seems, in the houses of the nobility."

The guest murmured appreciatively. Inkspot uncurled himself and sat up. He blinked, yawned, and began to wash his face, sitting in the middle of the hearth rug, insignificant and unobtrusive.

With a step as noiseless as Inkspot's own, the butler entered with the tray, a tall, suave figure with a lean, intelligent face sallow above his black clothes. Inkspot stopped washing his face and stared at the newcomer.

A strangled cry broke from the butler; the tray wavered in his hands, and a cup crashed to the floor. "Take it away! Take it away!" the man's face was a sick yellow, and he stood shuddering, with the tray rattling in his hands.

"Why, what's the matter?" His mistress was on her feet. "It's the kitten! Winnie, take it away—quickly!"

Winnie jumped up, plucked the innocent Inkspot from the rug, and scurried from the room. The butler put the tray down and mopped his damp face.

"Forgive me, madam. I do beg you to excuse it. It's cats, madam; I can't abide them. I'm most deeply sorry. It shan't occur again, madam—that is, if the cat keeps away."

"Very well, then, Jeffries. That's all," said his mistress hastily, and the butler stepped, a tall, quick shadow, through the heavy curtains and out of the room.

"Well!" said Winnie's mother. "Did you ever see anything so perfectly weird?"

"Oh, but it's quite well known—that horror of cats," said her guest, leaning forward animatedly. "There are people simply born that way, it seems."

That sealed Inkspot's doom. When Winnie stole up from the basement where, upon a pile of kindling, she had sat fearfully cuddling her pet, it was to hear Inkspot's banishment pronounced. She pleaded vainly, the kitten dangling limp and willing in her arms, her tears falling on his small black head, so that he twitched his ears once or twice in protest. "The cat must go," decreed her mother. And Uncle George dropped it outside and closed the heavy front door upon it where it stood, mewing unhappily, in the snow that was beginning to fill the winter night.

All night the wind cried around the house, blowing the snow in drifts between the pillars, fumbling at the shutters with icy fingers. Waking in the night, Winnie heard it, and heard, under her window, a faint and miserable mewing. She cried a little, piteously, into her pillow, there in the dark, and then went off to sleep again. But Inkspot prowled still around and around the unrelenting house, his fur blown the wrong way by cruel cold fingers of the wind. Dawn, breaking bleakly upon a world that the wearied wind had left numb with cold, found him crouched in the woodpile, in the damp straw that once had been a happy cradle. But the big sleek side that had warmed him was gone now; there was only the shut kitchen door that he watched with a forlorn stare, waiting hopefully.

And when it opened, Inkspot was there in a bound, crying his thin cry joyously, looking up with beseeching round green eyes in a baby face. Jeffries, in the doorway, sprang aside and slammed the door in the kitten's nose. For a long time Inkspot lingered, mournfully complaining, but no one came, and the door never opened, and after a while he went away, forlornly, into the world to see what he could find.

So Inkspot became an outcast, an Ishmael of the alleys. He lived on pickings from ash cans and dump piles; his coat grew mangy from bad food, and his green eyes wild and frightened. Crouching by a dust bin, licking an empty salmon can, he would bolt at a footstep, in the terror he had learned from harsh experience. He did not grow very fast, poorly nourished as he was, and he became daily thinner. Nothing could have been more insignificant than the superfluous black kitten that nevertheless managed to cling to life, unwanted and unhappy. Often he returned to the home of his brief happiness, for his hope was hard to kill, but always he was chased away, and once, when the sallow face of Jeffries looked down on him from the pantry window, he fled in terror.

Yet he returned once more. It was in the night, a night of black and bitter frost, with a great moon looking coldly on the world, when the old longing for remembered comfort came strongly back upon him. Over the frozen ruts of lane and alleyway he trotted, till he saw the white pillars of the house that had been home shining and stately in the moonlight. But Inkspot did not take the box-lined path that led to them, to the big house door. He knew now that door would never open to him. Yet with its picture of the dancing fire making a dim warmness in his kitten mind, he prowled miserably and hopelessly around the side of the house, looking up with eyes that glittered in the moonlight at the blank windows. And then, turning the corner, he stopped and stared. There was a black shadow there under one of the ground-floor windows, and the window was

open. He could hear the shadowy figure whispering; despite his fear he drew alertly nearer, drawn by that open window. In it, by the moon's light, he saw the face of Jeffries. Something brightly shining—the silver tray Inkspot knew—passed through the window to the man on the ground, who stooped and put it softly in the sack at his feet.

"That's about the last of the stuff," Jeffries was softly saying. "Now I'll fetch the rope, and you can come in and tie me and gag me."

The man under the window nodded silently, and Jeffries vanished from the window. In that instant the starved and shivering kitten ran to the window and leaped in, unseen, unsuspecting, and eager.

Despite the cold air from the open window, there was blessed warmth, and Inkspot's heart leaped up within him. There was a footfall in the dark room, and a whisper, and Inkspot, who bore no grudges, who looked on all in this haven as friends, ran with a little chirp to the shadowy figure and warmly, with his whole wriggling body, caressed the approaching ankle.

A terrible, uncontrollable yell broke from the throat of Jeffries. The shadow that had been darkening the moonlit window dropped from the sill, and its footfalls sounded in noisy haste down the path. A voice called upstairs; there were running feet. And when the door opened with a flood of light, the bewildered Inkspot looked up, blinking, to see crowding figures in the doorway, as bewildered as he, staring at Jeffries where he crouched against the wall shuddering and shrinking before the small, black, anxious kitten who sat in the middle of the floor between him and escape.

* * *

The next time there were guests for dinner, a crisply aproned maid brought in the silver service. At the sight, Inkspot, sleek and fattened, rose from the hearth rug waving his tail with an assured and lordly mien, and strolled to the table. Winnie's mother poured a fragile saucer full from the cream pitcher.

"Isn't he the dearest little creature?" she said fondly. "And do you know, he's a little hero! Let me tell you . . ."

But Inkspot, crouched greedily over the saucer, understood not a word. He only knew that somehow miraculously, he was wanted at last.

* * * * *

"Inkspot," by Louise Redfield Peattie. Published September 16, 1930, in The Youth's Instructor. *Reprinted by permission of Joe Wheeler (P.O. Box 1246, Conifer, CO 80433) and Review and Herald Publishing Association, Hagerstown, MD. Louise Redfield Peattie (1900–1960) married the well-known writer, Donald Culross Peattie (1898–1964), of Chicago. Both wrote and published prolifically, in many cases as coauthors.*

KING AND THE PRINCESS

-Jack O'Brien-

They still shake their heads up in the Northwest, telling the story of two devoted friends—one of the strangest such tales ever told.

* * *

The King lay outstretched in the warm sun on the east side of the cabin.

At times his legs jerked as he dreamed of rabbits racing through the tall grass. The Princess eyed him from the corner, then hobbled over, squatted down, and playfully whacked the King on the nose with her wooden leg. He awoke violently, sat up; then, seeing who had annoyed him, yawned and stretched again. The Princess curled up between his paws.

Sounds crazy, doesn't it? Kings and cabins. Lying in the sun, dreaming of rabbits. Princesses with wooden legs. Well, I'd like to tell you the strange story of this particular King and this particular Princess.

Up in the big timber country of the Northwest, Dad Wilson and his son, Bob, built and maintained a hunting lodge. Bob and his dad were both first-class woodsmen. Their cabin was located in what is perhaps the finest hunting and fishing country in the whole United States, and men from all over the country used to go there for their vacations.

One rainy afternoon Bob came into the big cabin room where his father was seated before the fire, reading. Young Bob had just paddled out from town and was wearing a raincoat. He tossed his hat on a chair and walked over to the table, a grin on his face.

"Look, Dad," he said.

His father's book dropped to his knees as Bob pulled out of his pockets two of the fattest, squirmiest pets ever seen in the Northwest. A kitten, black as night with a single white star on her forehead, and a puppy, so fat he fell in a heap when he tried to walk.

"Where in the world did you get them, Son?" exclaimed Dad Wilson.

"I got them from Mrs. Round at the boardinghouse in town. They're moving south, so they turned them over to me. Watch."

Bob put out his finger.

The kitten, not at all frightened after its curious ride in a raincoat pocket, leaped daintily upward, back arched and tail straight in the air, then minced sideways until near enough to pounce upon the pointing finger.

The pup, not to be outdone, rumbled into action like a baby truck, plowing across the oilcloth on stomach as well as feet, bringing himself up with a plop against Bob's hand, one huge paw planted across the kitten's neck.

With a squeal the kitten pulled her head out from beneath the paw and then, with all the spirit of a bantam fighter, slapped the clumsy puppy across the face with one front paw. That was the signal for a free-for-all. Around the floor the two of then tumbled, locked in fierce combat, biting each other without effect, for tiny teeth could not pierce the thick fur that grew on each small body. Bob and his father roared at their antics.

That was the first appearance of the pair and the beginning of their curious friendship. Bob named the puppy King, and dubbed the kitten Princess. Everyone thought the names most appropriate.

The two youngsters thrived and grew rapidly. King, of course, was destined to become a big dog and soon towered over little Princess. But the difference was in size only. Princess had the pep of a small tiger and battled King around the

floor, across the porch, and
out on the ground wherever
she saw him. And he loved
it! He never grew rough with
her, seeming to understand
the great difference and advantage he held in strength.

The King would often lie on his side with half-open eyes and
feign sleep. The Princess, noiseless as a drifting feather, would
creep closer and closer, maneuvering like a dark shadow until she
reached an advantageous point from which to pounce upon her
pal. Then down she'd come and around they'd thresh, King's big
paws exerting just enough pressure to hold her and his long jaws
clamped about her in mock ferocity, while the Princess yowled as
though she were being killed.

When he released her, she would spank him across the nose
and scramble away, leaping to the mantel. There she'd sit, calmly eyeing King, who raged beneath her, daring her to come down. She'd come
down in her own sweet time, sometimes landing on his back. Then, while he
whirled and raced about the place in sheer delight, the Princess clung to his thick
fur like a monkey.

That fall during the hunting season, a party of three came up from Chicago,
among them Doctor Mason, a famous surgeon. I was staying there, too, on a surveying job in the neighborhood.

One night after supper as we sat before the fire talking, we heard a low wail
like the sobbing of a child. King, who had been dozing in front of the fire, came
to his feet like a flash and was at the door, Bob right behind him. We knew the
wail. It was the Princess.

In a few moments Bob reappeared, bearing the black cat in his arms. King
pranced at his side, head high, whining at the burden the man bore. We stood
aside as he laid the Princess gently on the table. Her right front paw was badly
mangled, and she whimpered in pain as Bob held her head and Doctor Mason
worked over her.

"Someone must have left a set trap beneath the porch steps," Bob explained. His lips were drawn tight as he spoke. "She hopped off the step and landed right in it."

Doctor Mason looked up and said briskly, "Get plenty of hot water. I've got my kit. I'll amputate. It's the only way to save her."

For the next hour the cabin room resembled a hospital. The Princess was put to sleep while King paced up and down the floor. Men spoke in whispers. Bob and I helped the doctor, and it was an education to watch him. Those fine, sure fingers, whose skill brought fees of thousands of dollars, flew about the mangled paw with as much dexterity and gentleness as though he were working on a baby.

Well, pretty soon it was all over, and the Princess was laid in a little box, strapped so that the wound would heal. Her leg had been amputated just above the joint.

"Unless infection sets in, she'll be all right," Doctor Mason explained.

"But how will she ever walk, Doctor?" Bob wanted to know.

The surgeon smiled. "I'll attend to that, Son, in the morning." And he did.

While all hands kept coming to Princess's bed, talking to her as though she were human, and King took up his post right beside the box, never leaving even for food, the doctor was busy whittling on a piece of hickory. When at last he'd finished, there was perfected and waiting for the Princess the neatest peg leg you would ever want to see.

But it was weeks before Princess was well enough to use it. When he was sure that the wound had healed, Doctor Mason fitted the peg leg into place with a little harness across her shoulder. It was awkward at first, and Princess had trouble getting around. Her first attempts were laughable, yet nobody laughed as they watched her. The first time she fell she looked up and cried. King walked over, picked her up with his teeth, and carefully carried her back to her box.

But as time went on she grew more accustomed to her leg, and it wasn't long before she was thumping about the place making life miserable for King again. She had a weapon now, for when she would slap his face with that peg

it would really sting, and he'd draw back and bark at her until the pain had gone.

And so life went on in the little cabin just as it always had until one day the sun was dimmed, and we smelled smoke. Standing on the porch we looked toward the east.

"Fires," muttered Dad. "Forest fires and bad. Think they'll reach us, Bob?" His son shook his head.

"There's no wind. They'll burn out before they get this far." Bob was wrong.

The wind came up, and the fire roared toward the cabin. It was about two o'clock at night when the alarm was shouted by one of the men. As we dressed hurriedly, the reflection from the flames danced on the inside walls. It was getting hot, and smoke was filling the room.

"Save what you can carry and get out," Dad ordered. So we packed what we could and ran down the road, never stopping till morning at the side of the lake. Then as we were having a quick breakfast, the King emerged from the brush, tired-looking and covered with ashes. We glanced at each other, knowing what had happened. His pal was gone. In our desperate haste, we had forgotten her. The big dog dropped down beside us and soon fell asleep.

Late that afternoon the fire burned out, and we started back, disheartened by the disaster. King alone seemed strangely happy. He raced ahead barking at us as though urging us on. Then he'd run back and leap up at Bob, trying to get him to hurry.

We came at last to the cabin clearing and saw one of these miracles that sometimes occur in the woods.

The shack was still standing, untouched by flame. The fire had swung down to a point right behind it; then perhaps the wind had died and the draft had ceased. Whatever had happened, the Wilson home was intact. We moved in again and set things in order.

But King was not to be silenced. Back and forth he ranged, between the door and Bob, whining and barking and pleading. At last the man gave in. Tossing aside a jacket he had started to mend, he called to me.

"Come on, Jack. This fellow has got something on his mind. Let's see what it is."

We went outside. The King, overjoyed, raced straight for the river bank. Stopping on the shore, he turned and waited until we came up. Then, satisfied that we were with him, he barked once and plunged into the stream. Bob and I watched in silent wonder.

In the middle of the stream—it wasn't very wide—was a small bar or sort of island. On the island stood the stump of a tree. It had been a splendid oak once, but lightning had cut it down, leaving a blistered fragment four feet high.

Straight to the island swam the King and crawled up on the sandy beach. He shook himself once, then trotted to the stump. Here he stopped, reared up on his hind legs and with his forefeet against the post, cocked his head to one side, looking down into the hollow. We watched, and what we saw made us want to shout. Slowly and with great dignity the white-starred face of the Princess rose from the little nest at the top of the stump, then her shoulders and peg-leg harness came into view.

For a long minute she looked straight at the King as though scolding him for being late. He waited without moving a muscle. At last the little black lady struggled to the edge of the nest, felt her way cautiously onto King's broad head, and clung to his neck. Steadily he lowered himself to his four feet, turned, and walked back to the river. He never even paused at the water's edge but moved steadily into the stream and swam toward us.

Perched gaily on his back, her tail lashing happily, her peg leg stuck securely behind the King's ear, Princess rode in state to the landing place in front of the cabin. Neither Bob nor I spoke as the dog walked sedately up to us. Wilson took the kitten from her perch and set her on the ground. Relieved of his burden, King lowered his nose toward her to assure himself of her safety. She banged him with her wooden leg and hobbled away toward the cabin, the big dog rocking along beside her.

Bob looked at me for a long time, a slow smile on his lips. At last he said, "No one can ever tell me that King didn't hide her out there. That's just the sort of stunt that Bucko would pull for a pal."

King and the Princess

* * * * *

"King and the Princess," by Jack [John Sherman] O'Brien. If anyone can provide knowledge of the heirs to the O'Brien estate, please relay this information to Joe Wheeler (P.O. Box 1246, Conifer, CO 80433). Jack O'Brien (1898-1938) wrote animal and outdoor stories and books for the popular market during the first half of the twentieth century.

Fraidy Cat

-Arthur Gordon-

She was only an alley cat, and he merely endured her—because he was a dog man. Then she came to him crying, begging him to do something. He did, but it wasn't enough.

* * *

We got her at the place for friendless or abandoned animals—a tiny gray-and-white kitten whose eyes were still blue. Just an alley cat, nameless, homeless, too young to lap milk from a saucer—we had to feed her with an eyedropper. She didn't like the strange new world in which she found herself. She hid under the bed and cried. We laughed and called her Fraidy Cat.

She soon got used to us, of course. She slept a lot and played games with balls of wadded paper. I never saw her chase her tail, as kittens are supposed to do. But she had a good time.

She had an even better time when we moved to the country. She was half-grown, then, and liked to stalk things in the tall grass behind the house. Twice she brought home a mouse for us to admire, and once a bird. Fortunately the bird wasn't hurt, so we took it away from her and let it go. She seemed to think

our distinction between mice and birds was pretty silly. Logically, she was right.

She was an aloof little beast in those days. I say "little" because she remained a very small cat. She didn't show much affection for anyone. In fact, if you tried to pet her when she wasn't in the mood, she would dig her claws in harder than was pleasant—or even bite. This didn't bother me, of course, because I am really a dog man. I can take cats or leave them alone.

We acquired a dog soon after we moved to the country, a friendly boxer named Major. Fraidy loathed him. For the first month or so, if he came too close, she would spit and rake his nose, leaving him hurt and bewildered. I was rather indignant about this—after all, I'm a dog man—and I slapped Fraidy once or twice for assaulting Major. "Who do you think you are?" I asked her. "Try to remember you're nothing but a cat!"

While she was still too young, in our opinion, for such goings-on, Fraidy decided to become a mother. When the time came, however, she didn't hide away like most cats; she stuck close to us. Maybe she had a hunch it was going to be tough. It was. There was only a single kitten, much too big. She couldn't handle it herself; I had to help her. It took all my strength, and I thought she would bite me, but she didn't. She just watched me, her yellow eyes glassy with pain. Afterwards, she licked my hand. But the kitten was born dead.

"Never mind, Fraidy," we said. "You'll have better luck next time."

For days she was gaunt and thin; she looked for the kitten everywhere. I believe she thought Major was responsible for its disappearance—all her old distrust of him came back, for a while. She got over that, but one thing she did not get over—her gratitude to me. She followed me from room to room, and if I sat down she would jump into my lap, put her forefeet on my chest, and stare into my face with the most soulful look imaginable.

"Typical woman," my wife said, laughing. "In love with her obstetrician."

"It's just misplaced maternal instinct," I said. "She'll get over it as soon as she has some kittens."

Nature, it seemed, had the same idea, because before very long Fraidy was pregnant again. We figured she would have at least two kittens this time. Smaller ones. We were very happy for her. She seemed sleepy and satisfied.

Then one day, not long ago, she developed a cough. We thought nothing of it; her appetite was good. She seemed somewhat lethargic, but after all, her time was almost due. Then, early yesterday morning, she came up from the kitchen where she slept and jumped on our bed. She curled up in my lap and looked at me. She meowed unhappily. "What's the matter with this fool cat?" I said. "What's she trying to tell us?"

All yesterday she didn't eat. She even refused water. In the evening, finally, I called a vet. There are good vets, I guess, and bad ones. This one—when he saw her—said it seemed to be just a cold. No fever. Nothing very wrong. That was yesterday.

This morning Fraidy Cat dragged herself upstairs again, but this time she couldn't jump onto the bed. She was too weak. The roof of her mouth was very pale; her eyes were glazed.

I telephoned another vet. It was Sunday morning, and early, but he said to bring her over. I did. He examined her carefully. He knew his business; you can always tell. "I'm sorry," he said. "Uterine infection. I'm afraid the kittens are dead."

"Can't you operate?" I said. "Can't you save her?"

He shook his head. "I could try. But it would just prolong things. She's pretty far gone now." He looked at my face. He was a kind man, and he loved animals. "I'd put her away," he said gently, "if I were you."

After a while I nodded my head.

"Now?" said the vet, "Or after you've gone?"

"I'll stay with her," I said.

He brought the hypodermic needle and the Nembutal. "It doesn't hurt," he said. "She'll go to sleep, that's all." The needle went home, quick and merciful.

She was just an ordinary alley cat. She had no pedigree, no clever tricks. But I remembered how she'd roll over on the path when we'd drive up in the car. I remembered how she loved to eat slivers of melon from our breakfast plates. I remembered how she liked to have her ears scratched, and how she licked my hand the day I had to hurt her so terribly, the day her kitten was born dead.

I stood there with my hand touching her so that perhaps she would not be

afraid. "It's all right, Fraidy," I said. "Go to sleep. Go to sleep." And at last she put her head down on her clean little paws and closed her eyes.

I felt blindly for my pocketbook. It wasn't there. "I haven't any money," I said. "I'll have to send it to you."

"That's all right," the vet said. "Don't bother."

I touched her ear for the last time and turned back to the door. It was a golden summer morning, calm, serene. Down in the meadow a gigantic willow tree made a burst of greenness against the sky.

I got in the car quickly and drove away. But not far down the road I stopped the car and put my forehead against the steering wheel and wept. Because she was such a little cat. Because she had tried to tell me that she was sick, that she was in trouble, and I hadn't helped her. Not until too late. And I felt the awful emptiness that comes from not knowing how much you love something until you have lost it.

* * * * *

"Fraidy Cat," by Arthur Gordon. Published in Gordon's A Touch of Wonder *(Old Tappan, N.J., 1974). Reprinted by permission of Pamela Gordon. During his long and memorable career, Arthur Gordon (1912–2002) edited such magazines as* Cosmopolitan, Good Housekeeping, *and* Guideposts. *He was the author of a number of best-selling books as well as several hundred short stories.*

"MIDSHIPMAN," THE CAT

-John Coleman Adams-

Midshipman lived over a hundred years ago, but thanks to this story, his memory lingers yet.

* * *

This is a true story about a real cat who, for aught I know, is still alive and following the sea for a living. I hope to be excused if I use the pronouns "who" and "he" instead of "which" and "it," in speaking of this particular cat, because although I know very well that the grammars all tell us that "he" and "who" apply to persons, while "it" and "which" apply to things, this cat of mine always seemed to us who knew him to be so much like a human being, that I find it unsatisfactory to speak of him in any other way. There are some animals of whom you prefer to say "he," just as there are persons whom you sometimes feel like calling "it."

The way we met this cat was after this fashion: It was back somewhere in the seventies, and a party of us were cruising east from Boston in the little schooner-yacht *Eyvor*. We had dropped into Marblehead for a day and a night, and some of the boys had gone ashore in the tender. As they landed on the wharf, they found a group of small boys running sticks into a woodpile, evidently on a hunt for something inside.

"What have you in there?" asked one of the yachtsmen.

"Nothin' but a cat," said the boys.

"Well, what are you doing to him?"

"Oh, pokin' him up! When he comes out we'll rock him," was the answer, in good Marblehead dialect.

"Well, don't do it anymore. What's the use of tormenting a poor cat? Why don't you take on somebody of your size?"

The boys slowly moved off, a little ashamed and a little afraid of the big yachtsman who spoke, and when they were well out of sight the yachtsmen went on, too, and thought no more about the cat they had befriended. But when they had wandered about the tangled streets of the town for a little while and paid the visits that all good yachtsmen pay—to the grocery and the post office and the apothecary's soda-fountain—they returned to the wharf and found their boat. Behold, there in the stern sheets sat the little gray-and-white cat of the woodpile! He had crawled out of his retreat and made straight for the boat of his champions. He seemed in no wise disturbed or disposed to move when they jumped on board, nor did he show anything but pleasure when they stroked and patted him. But when one of the boys started to put him ashore, the plucky little fellow showed his claws. No sooner was he set on his feet at the edge of the wharf than he turned about and jumped straight back into the boat.

"He wants to go yachting," said one of the party, whom we called the Bos'n.

"Ye might as wal take the cat," said a grizzly old fisherman standing on the wharf. "He doesn't belong to anybody, and ef he stays here the boys'll worry him t' death."

"Let's take him aboard," said the yachtsmen. "It's good luck to have a cat on board ship."

Whether it was good luck to the ship or not, it was very clear that the cat saw it meant good luck to *him* and curled himself down in the bottom of the boat with a look that meant business. Evidently he had thought the matter all over and made

up his mind that these were the kind of people he wanted to live with, and, being a Marblehead cat, it made no difference to him whether they lived afloat or ashore; he was going where they went, whether they wanted him or not. He had heard the conversation from his place in the woodpile and had decided to show his gratitude by going to sea with his protectors. By casting his lot with theirs he was paying them the highest compliment of which a cat is capable. It would have been the height of impoliteness not to recognize his distinguished appreciation. So he was allowed to remain in the boat and was taken off to the yacht.

Upon his arrival there, a council was held, and it was unanimously decided that the cat should be received as a member of the crew. And as we were a company of amateur sailors, sailing our own boat, each man having his particular duties, it was decided that the cat should be appointed midshipman and should be named after his position. So he was at once, and ever after, known as Middy. Everybody took a great interest in him, and he took an impartial interest in everybody—though there were two people on board to whom he made himself particularly agreeable. One was the quiet, kindly professor, the captain of the *Eyvor;* the other was Charlie, our cook and only hired hand. Middy, you see, had a seaman's true instinct as to the official persons with whom it was his best interest to stand well.

It was surprising to see how quickly Middy made himself at home. He acted as if he had always been at sea. He was never seasick, no matter how rough it was or how uncomfortable any of the rest of us were. He roamed wherever he wanted, all over the boat. At meal times he came to the table with the rest, sat up on a valise, and lapped his milk and took what bits of food were given him, as if he had eaten that way all his life. When the sails were hoisted it was his especial joke to jump upon the main-gaff and be hoisted with it, and once he stayed on his perch till the sail was at the masthead. One of us had to go aloft and bring him down. When we had come to anchor and everything was snug for the night, he would come on deck and scamper out on the main-boom and race from there to the bowsprit end as fast as he could gallop, then climb, monkey-fashion, half-way up the masts and drop back to the deck or dive down into the cabin and run riot among the berths.

One day, as we were jogging along under a pleasant southwest wind and everybody was lounging and dozing after dinner, we heard the Bos'n call out, "Stop that, you fellows!" and a moment after, "I tell you, quit! Or I'll come up and make you!"

We opened our lazy eyes to see what was the matter, and there sat the Bos'n, down in the cabin, close to the companionway, the tassel of his knitted cap coming nearly up to the combings of the hatch, and on the deck outside sat Middy, digging his claws into the tempting yarn and occasionally going deep enough to scratch the Bos'n's scalp.

When night came and we were all settled down in bed, it was Middy's almost invariable custom to go the rounds of all the berths, to see if we were properly tucked in, and to end his inspection by jumping into the captain's bed, treating himself to a comfortable nest there among the blankets and curling himself down to sleep. It was his own idea to select the captain's berth as the only proper place in which to turn in.

But the most interesting trait in Middy's character did not appear until he had been a week or so on board. Then he gave us a surprise. It was when we were lying in Camden harbor. Everybody was going ashore to take a tramp among the hills, and Charlie, the cook, was coming too, to row the boat back to the yacht.

Middy discovered that he was somehow "getting left." Being a prompt and very decided cat, it did not take him long to make up his mind what to do. He ran to the low rail of the yacht, put his forepaws on it, and gave us a long, anxious look. Then as the boat was shoved off he raised his voice in a plaintive mew. We waved him a goodbye, chaffed him pleasantly, and told him to mind the anchor and have dinner ready when we got back.

That was too much for his temper. As quick as a flash he had dived overboard and was swimming like a water spaniel, after the dinghy!

That was the strangest thing we had ever seen in all our lives! We were quite used to elephants that could play at seesaw and to horses that could fire cannons, to learned pigs and to educated dogs, but a cat that of his own accord would take to the water like a full-blooded Newfoundland was a little beyond anything we had ever heard of. Of course the boat was stopped, and Middy was taken aboard,

drenched and shivering, but perfectly happy to be once more with the crew. He had been ignored and slighted, but he had insisted on his rights, and as soon as they were recognized he was quite contented.

Of course, after that we were quite prepared for anything that Middy might do. And yet he always managed to surprise us by his bold and independent behavior. Perhaps his most brilliant performance was a visit he paid a few days after his swim in Camden harbor.

We were lying becalmed in a lull of the wind off the entrance to Southwest Harbor. Near us, perhaps a cable's length away, lay another small yacht, a schooner hailing from Lynn. As we drifted along on the tide, we noticed that Middy was growing very restless. Presently we found him running along the rail and looking eagerly toward the other yacht. What did he see—or smell—over there that so interested him? It could not be the dinner, for they were not then cooking. Did he recognize any of his old chums from Marblehead? Perhaps there were some cat friends of his on the other craft. Ah, that was it! There they were on the deck, playing and frisking together—two kittens! Middy had spied them and was longing to take a nearer look. He ran up and down the deck, mewing and snuffing the air. He stood up in his favorite position when on lookout, with his forepaws on the rail. Then, before we realized what he was doing, he had plunged overboard again, and was making for the other boat as fast as he could swim! He had attracted the attention of her company, and no sooner did he come up alongside than they prepared to welcome him. A fender was lowered, and when Middy saw it he swam toward it, caught it with his forepaws, clambered along it to the gunwale, and in a twinkling was over the side and on the deck getting acquainted with the strange kittens.

How they received him I hardly know, for by that time our boat was alongside to claim the runaway. And we were quite of the mind of the skipper of the *Winnie L.*, who said, as he handed our bold midshipman over the side, "Well, that beats all I've ever seen!"

Only a day or two later Middy was very disobedient when we were washing decks one morning. He trotted about in the wet till his feet were drenched and then retired to dry them on the white spreads of the berths below. That was quite too much for the captain's patience. Middy was summoned aft, and, after a sound scolding, was hustled into the dinghy that was moored astern, and shoved off to the full length of her painter. The punishment was a severe one for Middy, who could bear anything better than exile from his beloved shipmates. So of course, he began to exercise his ingenious little brain to see how he could escape. Well under the overhang of the yacht he spied, just about four inches out of water, a little shoulder of the rudder. That was enough for him. He did not stop to think whether he would be any better off there. It was a part of the yacht, and that was home. So overboard he went, swam for the rudder, scrambled onto it, and began howling piteously to be taken on deck again. And, being a spoiled and much-indulged cat, he was soon rescued from his uncomfortable roosting place and restored to favor.

I suppose I shall tax your powers of belief if I tell you many more of Middy's doings. But truly he was a strange cat, and you may as well be patient, for you will not soon hear of his equal. The captain was much given to rifle practice and used to love to go ashore and shoot at targets. On one of his trips he allowed Middy to accompany him, for the simple reason, I suppose, that Middy decided to go and got on board the dinghy when the captain did. Once ashore, the marksman selected a large rock as a rest for his rifle, and opened fire upon his target. At the first shot or two Middy seemed a little surprised, but showed no disposition to run away. After the first few rounds, however, he seemed to have made up his mind that since the captain was making all that racket it must be entirely right and proper and nothing about which a cat need bother his head in the least. So, as if to show how entirely he confided in the captain's judgment and good intentions, that imperturbable cat calmly lay down, curled up, and went to sleep in the shade of the rock over which the captain's rifle was blazing and cracking about once every two minutes. If anybody was ever acquainted with a cooler or more self-possessed cat, I should be pleased to hear the particulars.

I wish that this chronicle could be confined to nothing but our shipmate's feats of daring and nerve. But, unfortunately, he was not always blameless in his conduct. When he got hungry he was apt to forget his position as midshipman

and to behave just like any cat with an empty stomach. Here is one of this cat midshipman's exploits. One afternoon, on our way home, we were working along with a headwind and sea toward Wood Island, a haven for many of the small yachts between Portland and the Shoals. The wind was light, and we

were a little late in making port. But as we were all agreed that it would be pleasanter to postpone our dinner till we were at anchor, the cook was told to keep things warm and wait till we were inside the port before he set the table. Now, his main dish that day was to be a fine piece of baked fish, and, unfortunately, it was nearly done when we gave orders to hold back the dinner. So he had closed the drafts of his little stove, left the door of the oven open, and turned into his bunk for a quiet doze—a thing which every good sailor does on all possible occasions, for a seafaring life is very uncertain in the matter of sleep, and one never quite knows when he will lose some, nor how much he will lose. So it is well to lay in a good stock of it whenever you can.

It seems that Middy was on watch, and when he saw Charlie fast asleep he undertook to secure a little early dinner for himself. He evidently reasoned with himself that it was very uncertain when we should have dinner and he'd better get his while he could. He quietly slipped down to the stove, walked coolly up to the oven, and began to help himself to baked haddock.

He must have missed his aim or made some mistake in his management of the business, and, by some lucky chance for the rest of us, waked the cook. For, the first we knew, Middy came flying up the cabin companionway, followed by a volley of shoes and spoons and pieces of coal, while we could hear Charlie, who was rather given to unseemly language when he was excited, using the strongest words in his dictionary about "that thief of a cat!"

"What's the matter?" we all shouted at once.

"Matter enough, sirs!" growled Charlie. "That little cat's eaten up half the fish! It'll be a miracle if you get any dinner tonight, sirs."

You may be very sure that Middy got a sound scolding for that trick, but I am afraid the captain forgot to deprive him of his rations as he threatened. He was much too kindhearted.

The very next evening Middy startled us again by a most remarkable display of coolness and courage. After a weary thrash to windward all day, under a provokingly light breeze, we found ourselves under the lee of the little promontory at Cape Neddick, where we cast anchor for the night. Our supply of water had run very low, and so, just after sunset, two of the party rowed ashore in the tender to replenish our water keg, and by special permission Middy went with them.

It took some time to find a well, and by the time the jugs were filled it had grown quite dark. When the fellows launched the boat for the return to the yacht, by some ill luck a breaker caught her and threw her back upon the beach. There she capsized and spilled out the boys, together with their precious cargo. In the confusion of the moment and the hurry of setting matters to rights, Middy was entirely forgotten, and when the boat again was launched, nobody thought to look for the cat. This time everything went well, and in a few minutes the yacht was sighted through the dusk. Then somebody happened to think of Middy! He was nowhere to be seen. Neither man remembered anything about him after the capsizing. There was consternation in the hearts of those unlucky sailors, for to lose Middy was almost like losing one of the crew.

But it was too late and too dark to go back and risk another landing on the beach. There was nothing to be done but to leave poor Middy to his fate, or at least to wait until morning before searching for him.

But just as the prow of the boat bumped against the fender on the yacht's quarter, out from under the stern-sheets came a wet, bedraggled, shivering cat, who leaped on board the yacht and hurried below into the warm cabin. In that moist adventure on the surf, Middy had taken care of himself, rescued himself

from a watery grave, got on board the boat as soon as she was ready, and sheltered himself in the warmest corner. All this he had done without the least outcry and without asking any help whatever. His self-reliance and courage were extraordinary.

Well, the pleasant month of cruising drew to a close, and it became a question what should be done with Middy. We could not think of turning him adrift in the cold world, although we had no fears but that so bright and plucky a cat would make a living anywhere. But we wanted to watch over his fortunes, and perhaps take him on the next cruise with us when he should have become more settled and dignified. Finally, it was decided that he should be boarded for the winter with an artist, a friend of one of our party. She wanted a studio cat and would be particularly pleased to receive so accomplished and traveled a character as Middy. So when the yacht was moored to the little wharf at Annisquam, where she always ended her cruises, and we were packed and ready for our journey to Boston, Middy was tucked into a basket and taken to the train. He bore the confinement with the same good sense which had marked all his life with us, though I think his feelings were hurt at the lack of confidence we showed in him. And, in truth, we were a little ashamed of it ourselves, and when once we were on the train somebody suggested that he be released from his prison just to see how he would behave. We might have known he would do himself credit. For when he had looked over his surroundings, peeped above the back of the seat at the passengers, taken a good look at the conductor, and counted the rest of the party to see that none of us was missing, Middy snuggled down upon the seat, laid his head upon the captain's knee, and slept all the way to Boston.

That was the last time I ever saw Middy. He was taken to his new boarding place in Boylston Street, where he lived very pleasantly for a few months and made many friends by his pleasing manners and unruffled temper. But I suppose he found it a little dull in Boston. He was not quite at home in his esthetic surroundings. I have always believed he sighed for the freedom of a sailor's life. He loved to sit by the open window when the wind was east, and seemed to be dreaming of faraway scenes. One day he disappeared. No trace of him was ever

found. A great many things may have happened to him. But I never could get rid of the feeling that he went down to the wharves and the ships and the sailors, trying to find his old friends, looking everywhere for the stanch little *Eyvor,* and, not finding her, I am convinced that he shipped out on some East Indiaman and is now a sailor cat on the high seas.

* * * * *

" 'Midshipman,' the Cat," by John Coleman Adams. Published August 1892 in St. Nicholas. *Text reprinted by permission of Joe Wheeler (P.O. Box 1246, Conifer, CO 80433). John Coleman Adams (1849–1922) was born in Malden, Massachusetts. Besides being a clergyman, he wrote a number of books and short stories during the second half of the nineteenth century and the early part of the twentieth.*

ALBERT

-Blythe Morley Brennan-

She bought him not knowing which of the squirming little bodies he was. She took him for granted, and he wet her couch until she mended her ways.
Finally, he was free to soar.

* * *

He was large. He was long-tailed. He was gray-striped. In general shape and coloring he looked like a million and one other cats that can be found in back alleys all over America and Europe. But he had one distinct physical characteristic that marked him out from all those other cats—and that was the striking, meditative quality of his enormous, round, lime-green eyes. Those eyes would train themselves on you, when he looked at you, with great intensity, and sometimes the lid of the left eye would lower in a surprising wink.

His eyes, however, were in no way remarkable when I first saw him one September day some fifteen years ago. At that time I was twenty-two years old, a single young woman living by myself in a little apartment in New York in Greenwich Village; he was six weeks old, shut up inside a cage in the foundling department of New York's famous Speyer Animal Hospital. He was one of a scruffy-looking litter of four kittens who were still with their mother. The whole lot of them, I gathered, had been rescued from the streets, and all of them, mother and kittens alike, were gray-striped and puny, with lackluster eyes and undistinguished fur. But they were the only kittens currently available at the Speyer Hospital, and I wanted, or thought I wanted, a kitten. To choose from such a group was impossible, so, leaving it up to chance, I pointed. The attendant picked up the one at which he thought I had pointed and deposited it in a cardboard carton. And that was that. Picking up the box in a gingerly manner, I walked homeward across lower Manhattan. There I placed the box in the middle of the floor, opened it, and lifted the kitten out.

He did not move very far but, mewing faintly, stood looking weakly about him. Removed from his mother and litter mates, he seemed even thinner and scruffier. The angular look of his elbows hinted at rickets. Still I did not have the sense to feel dubious; I knew very little about cats, and I had an optimistic, youthful notion that they could survive almost anything, that vitamins and a couple of worm pills would work miracles within a week or so. Envisioning that this waif would soon turn into a plump, glossy, lively kitten, I gave him some milk and set about thinking up a name for him. Somehow his pompous, puny manner suggested the name of Albert, and Albert he became.

He learned his name quite soon, but he never turned into a plump, glossy, lively kitten.

Concerning his kittenhood, in fact, perhaps the less that is said the better. For he never had any real kittenhood at all. He was not at all playful, not at all clean, and not at all cute. He slept, he ate, he vomited, and he slept. In between times I took him to the vet. Worms were the major enemy, and they nearly killed him. I barely realized it at the time. I had acquired him because I wanted company, I thought, while I was not involved in my other activities. But during that year my activities became much more frenetic than I had anticipated; they consisted of running around looking for theater jobs, occasionally doing some very small theater job, writing, working at Macy's when I ran out of money, falling in and out of love, and generally enjoying and abusing the privilege of being what I thought was grown-up. In and among these activities, I tended to

look on Albert as a form of interior decoration who willfully refused to be deco-
rative. I certainly wasn't paying enough attention to him, and when I was paying
attention to him, I was subjecting him to a theory.

The theory was that cats should be brought up like dogs. Train a cat like a
dog, I philosophized; talk to him, give him a decent name instead of degrading
him by calling him "Kitty-Kitty," teach him tricks, and companionship would
follow as the night the day. Well, up to a certain point the theory was sound—
but only up to a point. It was left to Albert himself to show me where the theory
went wrong. This he did when he finally began to gain vitality at the age of six or
seven months.

So began the era of wet bedclothes.

Looking back on that era, I don't quite know how we survived it. By all
rights, when Albert began to express his irritation with me by wetting regularly in
the exact center of the studio couch, I should probably have despaired and given
him away. But at that particular time I was mildly busy, morning, noon, and
night, stage-managing an off-Broadway production of *The Return of the Native,*
and in my preoccupation, happily, I had no time to give Albert away or even to
consider the possibility of giving him away. I barely had time to chase him, catch
him, and punish him with a folded newspaper as I would have punished a puppy.
It was a frenzied period while it lasted. But then it ended almost as suddenly as it
had begun. In the first place, *The Return of the Native* finally opened and immediately afterwards closed. And in the second place, having more time at home, I
suddenly began to observe Albert and to come to my senses. I stopped treating
him like a dog and began to treat him like an individual. I stopped punishing
him. I petted him more. I played with him more. And it worked. His behavior
improved, and the couch remained dry.

So spring came on—April and May and June—and Albert flourished. He
looked full-grown by now, but he continued to grow larger. He leaped. He gal-
loped. He gamboled. From the floor to the easy chair to the marble mantel to the
eight-foot-high top of the built-in closet, he would leap in one long flowing
movement; then around and down again, by way of the studio couch. He learned
all the kitten games that he had ignored when he was younger—chasing ping-

pong balls or crumpled bits of paper. He took new, delirious interest in catnip mice, those martinis of catdom, and became so addicted to them that in time I began to mass-produce them. Presently, one whole drawer of my desk was turned into an assembly line for making catnip mice. Meanwhile, he was exploring every corner and every level of the apartment, including the linen shelves, and he was exploring every object in the apartment, too. Now whatever was movable—a lipstick left on the bureau or a pencil left on the desk—he moved. Whatever was openable—small drawers, or the door to the icebox—he learned how to open. Whatever was awakeable—his owner, comfortably asleep at six in the morning— he learned how to awake.

He had various methods for waking me. There was, of course, the rough method; as I lay in bed a large form would land on my shoulder, a delicate cool nose and a prickly array of whiskers would be thrust into my face. But he found that this method did not always work. I developed defenses; I dove under the bedclothes and ignored him. As a result, after a while he invented a subtler approach. By my couch, as I slept, I kept on a shelf the usual bed table impedimenta—alarm clock, ashtray, wristwatch, eyeglasses. He found eventually that the very best way to rouse me was to sit on the shelf and delicately move these objects around with his paw. He would move an insignificant object first—an ashtray or a stray pencil. If that did not work, he would move the more valuable objects— my eyeglasses, my watch. Invariably, by the time my glasses or my wristwatch had been shifted to the edge of the shelf, I would be wide awake, reaching out in fury to rescue the object.

Most of his games and tricks were invented during this period when he was eight months to a year old. It was a gentle and a lively and a home-centered period. He was learning many things that he could do inside the apartment, and a few things that he could not do. He learned, for instance, that he could not fly. I remember very well the moment when he discovered this limitation. He had happily chased a housefly from one end of the apartment to the other. Then it flew up to the chandelier. Albert leaped once for it and failed. He leaped a second time and failed. Then, baffled, he sat down under the chandelier. He looked at me over his shoulder and queried me with a delicate meowing sound. There was a sadness

in his eyes and in his voice. "What?" he seemed to be saying. "Cats can't fly?"

"No," I said, "it is a pity, but there are some things that cats cannot do."

Dejectedly he looked back at the fly. But he had learned. He was a realist; he never again tried to fly up to the chandelier.

Even at that moment, however, he was on the verge of learning that cats can do much more interesting things than fly. His home-centered period was nearly over. He was about to take on the great outer world.

* * *

The outer world lay beyond our windows. These windows, two in number, were at the end of my long narrow apartment. Facing south, at the height of four stories, they commanded a splendid miscellaneous view of chock-ablock back gardens, lush ailanthus trees, higgledy-piggledy buildings, and random rooftops. Outside the left-hand window was a sheer drop to the paved backyard of our building, and outside the right-hand window was a fire escape, which zig-zagged downward two stories to a flat roof. Off the end of the roof, beyond fences, lay the sleek, well-kept gardens of Waverly Place. The houses of Waverly Place, chiefly handsome old four- and five-story brownstones, formed part of the skyline, and beyond them were the buildings, some tall, some short, some elegant, some dilapidated, that clustered around the west side of Washington Square.

But it was not the view of the skyline but the traffic on our fire escape that began to draw Albert toward this outer world. Traffic was cats, perhaps one cat a day, and pigeons, perhaps one pigeon a week, and sparrows, perhaps three sparrows a day. Even more than the sparrows and the pigeons, the cats interested him. He began to spend hours at the fire-escape window, staring out through the glass or through the wire screen that I had installed to keep him indoors. He turned sometimes and asked me in his modulated cat voice to let him out, but I was afraid to do so. Then one day he gave up asking and went to the other window, which I had foolishly left open. There, before I could stop him, he wavered on the sill like a novice diver on a high board. One second later he launched himself across five feet of void toward the fire escape. He made it, of course, landing precariously, breathlessly between two of the vertical railings, which were six inches apart. Evidently he knew his own capabilities better than I did. Nonetheless my heart as I watched him stopped dead for a long moment.

After that I did not try to keep him indoors. Watching him at first like an anxious mother, I let him out for longer and longer periods. And bold as a Boy Scout and twice as bright-eyed he began setting off down the fire escape day after day to meet the other cats and to explore the world of Greenwich Village.

I worried at first about his coming back, but I soon found that he could be trusted to come when I called him. I felt rather foolish at first, leaning out of my lofty tenement window to yodel "Albert!" But presently I began to feel proud, for my musical efforts would always be rewarded, eventually, by the sight of that large gray animal abandoning his freedom, bounding across the roof beneath me and leaping up the fire escape to join me purringly at the window. I do not know why he was so obedient about coming because in other situations he was, like most cats, quite consistently disobedient. But in answering my call when he was out-doors, as though he knew that this was serious business, he never disobeyed if he could help it.

Finally, I let him come and go pretty much as he wished. And when I did this we entered a new phase in our relationship. Now that Albert had been given his freedom it seemed as though, little by little, he could risk being more openly affectionate with me; he could occasionally abandon his feline attitude of total independence. And so our friendship grew stronger.

Two things brought this home to me during the first two years of his life. The first, I fear, was almost a psychological disaster for Albert. The second was a triumph.

In the first case, I had left him alone overnight while I went out of town on a Saturday and Sunday with an old college friend. I had done this with Albert before, and he had always come through such overnights in good shape. But this time, through no one's fault, I was gone for several days and was unable to get back to the apartment until the following Wednesday. My friend Nancy came down with a virus infection that shot her temperature up alarmingly, and I could not leave her. But I was able to phone my superintendent on Eighth Street, and I arranged to

have his daughter feed Albert and give him water, so I did not worry too much about him.

As soon as Nancy was better, however, I rushed into New York on a flying visit to Albert.

What I found when I opened the apartment door convinced me for all time that cats are not as indifferent to people as people say they are. No furry form bounded to greet me. No welcoming meow sounded from anywhere. On the floor near the doorway, an obviously fresh meal of cat food stood untouched. With a thud of fear in my throat I shut the door and stepped farther into the apartment. I found Albert then on one corner of the couch, curled up in glazed-eyed misery. So deep was his sense of having been abandoned, so far had he retreated into himself, that he would not believe at first that I had really returned. Only little by little, like someone suffering from the effects of shock, did he emerge from his stupor. For over half an hour I petted him, held him, and comforted him. Heartrendingly then, when he was finally convinced that I had come back, he returned to life and indicated his joy at seeing me. Then we had a game, and then he thirstily drank and hungrily ate, and then, from then on, he was all right.

It was not just I personally who had deserted him, of course, but all humankind. I would have expected the superintendent's child—a stout, reliable-seeming child of fourteen—to have petted Albert a bit, played with him a bit, when she fed him. She hadn't. She had fed him, but that was all. And food wasn't enough.

The withdrawn, glazed look that I saw in Albert's eyes that day I have seen many times since. I have seen it in the eyes of stray cats cowering for shelter in tenement backyards or under the abutments of Manhattan bridges; in the eyes of cats left alone in cages in animal foundling homes; and, although I hate to acknowledge it, even in the eyes of cats who are nominally pets, whose owners keep them for some picayune reason—perhaps to amuse a three-year-old—whose owners feed them and do not love them. The world abounds in worse tragedies, I know, and I do not wish to sound oversentimental in describing the plight of cats. But many people do not seem to be aware that all pet animals need love.

Albert helped to teach me this, in that year when I was twenty-three, and he helped to teach me that the absence of love is a form of death—even for an animal.

The second critical episode in those first two years of Albert's life occurred at night and occurred outdoors. Albert was about two years old, and I was, finally, flourishingly settled in a job that netted a steady income, a theater office job. Beef kidney for Albert and lamb chops for myself were found more often inside our icebox, and a steady, cheerful stream of theater friends—young actors, actresses, would-be scenic designers and would-be directors—flowed through our apartment when I was home. Nonetheless, despite the occasional traffic of sociability, a good part of the time I was away in the evenings, for my job often required me to attend play readings or studio productions of new plays. Albert, by then, was used to being allowed outdoors on his own, by night as well as by day, so I would leave the window open for him if the weather permitted it. He came and went as he pleased, and he continued to be virtuous about answering my summons. When I returned late in the evening, a single low-voiced call or whistle would always bring him bounding velvet-footed through the darkness across the fences and roofs of the night. After he had visited with me he might go out again and not return until dawn; but invariably he responded to my summons, and then I could feed him a late snack and go to sleep knowing that he was all right.

One winter midnight, however, when I returned home and called, and called, no gray form materialized below me on the fire escape. I stood by the window and slowly began to realize that I was in a predicament. An animal owner who lives in the country or the suburbs can go out to look for his animal if it is lost or in trouble. But the citified outdoors where Albert had vanished was beyond my reach. I could not climb over fire escapes and rooftops, or try to penetrate walled gardens and barred alleys, to seek my missing pet. Was there, I tried to figure out, anything else I could do?

Then, ever so faintly, I heard Albert's voice, a single plaintive *meow.* Startled into action, I hurried to get my flashlight. Throwing the window open, I stepped out onto the fire escape and trained the flashlight's beam into the darkness below me. I examined roofs, fences, and as much of nearby gardens as I could. Every so

often Albert meowed, even more plaintively, but also, now, hopefully. There was something strange about trying to locate that disembodied meow. It seemed to come from midair, in fact from somewhere as high as I was—four flights high. I began to sweep the flashlight wildly to illuminate the vacant dark above the ground. Higher and higher I swept it. Then, as though switched on by electricity, two glowing bits of green light answered me, hanging midair in the night about fifty feet away and nearly at my own eye level.

Was it possible? Were those two green lights Albert's eyes?

"Meow!" A really loud response this time—an affirmative, desperate YES.

A tree. He was up a tree. Of course. And of course he was on the top branch of the highest tree in the area.

It looked, moreover, like a very thin branch.

I stood on the fire escape as though lead had been dropped into my shoes. If there was comedy in this situation—and I was aware that there was—I did not want to recognize it. Albert was my own darling cat. Let other people laugh at other people's cats up other trees. It was a cold night, too, below freezing. It was not a night for leaving any creature helpless and motionless in the open air. But cold as it was, I did not think I dared to call out the SPCA or the fire department at such an hour. And even if it were not one o'clock in the morning, how could the fire department or the SPCA ever set up an extension ladder in that cloistered, higgledly-piggledy backyard area?

I played the flashlight up and down the tree. Its roots were in a closed yard on Waverly Place, but its trunk passed within six inches of the high back fence that belonged to my own building. Right by that fence, in the backyard of my building, was a peculiar rock garden built by some long-gone, overimaginative superintendent. This rock-garden structure was five or six feet high, and perhaps if I climbed up on it I could evaluate the situation better.

I put on a heavier coat, changed my shoes to sneakers, and went downstairs. From the ground-floor hallway I stepped into the backyard as noiselessly as I could. As I shut the door behind me, darkness and cold enveloped me. The winter stars shone dimly above the leafless trees and beyond the sooty rooftops. In all of the silent nearby buildings, almost all of the lights were out. Even though this was Greenwich Village, with a stay-up-late reputation, most people in this neighborhood were obviously asleep. Please God, they would stay asleep—especially my superintendent, the one with the stout daughter; his windows were just a few feet away from me, and he might well mistake me for a prowler.

These thoughts flashed through my mind within an instant as I crossed toward Albert's tree. Then as I looked upward, the thoughts disappeared, and nothing was left in my mind except the problem at hand.

The problem looked insoluble. Albert was in a real fix. From high, high up where he was silhouetted against the stars, he looked down at me in fright. He was clinging to a minute branch where it made a crotch at the treetop, and he looked enormously insecure as well as tiny and far away. Below him the bark of the ailanthus tree was smooth and thin-looking, and the trunk was relatively branchless, so there would be few resting places for him even if I were able to get him to try to clamber down. *Oh, Albert, you fool,* I wanted to say, *however did you get up there?* That was silly, for I knew pretty well how he must have gotten up there. Something—a barking dog, a bottle-throwing human—had frightened him. And frightened cats, I had begun to learn, can accomplish quite unbelievable feats. Under the influence of fear they can scale twelve-foot walls, rip their way out of the grasp of a circus strongman, or flash to the top of bare poles. But when the immediate fright has left them, repeating such a feat is difficult. And coming down a tall pole or tree in cold blood—since they have to come down backwards—is nearly impossible.

But it did me no good to know these facts as I stood shivering in the dark backyard. I forced myself to move. Scrambling among odd, concreted clusters of stone, I climbed uneasily up on the rock garden. From there I could hang on to the top of the fence for balance, and I could touch the trunk of the tree where Albert was lodged.

"Albert," I said in what I hoped was a low and matter-of-fact voice, "Albert, you dear fool, you're in a spot, yes, but it's not impossible. Just try coming down backwards, slowly. I'm right here. You can make it."

I talked gently for quite a while. He talked back, first contradicting me, then pleading with me. Our conversation went on for about twenty minutes. Then

finally—after he had made a last desperate moaning sound that clearly meant, "Well-all-right-but-if-I-slip-and-die-it'll-be-all-your-fault," he started down.

I sweated every inch of it. The bark was too meager to give his claws purchase; bits of it flaked off and showered down on me as he struggled to hold on. But I kept talking him down—as much perhaps for my own sake as for his. "All right, fine, now there's a branch two feet below you. Good fellow, that's it. Now there's a knothole near your left hind foot . . ." and strangely it seemed to help.

After a century of time he slid down the last slippery length of trunk, and I reached up and caught him in my arms.

As I held him against me he was trembling; so was I. For several minutes we both remained there, unable to move. I felt as though I had climbed down that tree myself. Then a damp nose butted against my chin, and through my arms I felt a vibration other than trembling. Raucously, gaspingly, Albert was purring, a rough and breathless purr of purest triumph.

That night came to seem like a landmark in our friendship, an inarticulate confirmation of mutual trust. It was also a landmark in Albert's mastery of the outside world. He never again got stuck up a tree; he had proved to himself that when he got up he could get down.

Still I think the conquering of the tree may have been minor to him compared with other crises of his youth. I had less to do with those other crises, but glancingly, from a distance, I was aware that they took place.

Other cats, for instance, were what he had originally gone outside to see. But other cats were not always so eager to see him as he was to see them.

Chief among these cats was an enormous, gaunt, tiger-striped tomcat whom I presently nicknamed the Bruiser. In general looks the Bruiser was a real thug of a cat, with heavy shoulders, chewed-up ears, and a grim and jowly face. He appeared to exist on random handouts from a restaurant on Waverly Place, but on the whole he was ownerless and afraid of people. When Albert was very young, the Bruiser had occasionally dared to stop at our windowsill, when the window was closed, and crouch there, glaring in through the glass at Albert. After a while Albert had learned to glare back. The glaring game could be carried on for hours, while each cat, in the back of his throat, manufactured that strange, wailing, growling, crooning sound that cats make and that, in its crescendo form, is alternatively the cry of the fight or the love duet.

In the beginning, in those glaring matches, Albert was always the first to lower his eyes. And in the beginning, when I first began to open the window for Albert to go out, Albert always came off second best when he encountered the Bruiser. Stepping out onto the fire escape, he soon learned to look around to see whether the Bruiser was nearby. For the Bruiser was top among the cats in the area. He was in effect the king of the cats, of all the cats who lived in this block between Eighth Street and Waverly Place. The roof downstairs was his special hangout, and if he happened to be sunning on the roof, let other cats beware.

I never completely figured out the strange relationship that in time grew up between Albert and the Bruiser. It seemed to be part love as well as part hate. Albert's sex may have influenced it, for he was not fully male, but neuter. When I had adopted Albert I had had to promise, as long as I was going to keep him in the city, to have him altered at the age of five or six months. The Speyer Hospital people know that it is almost impossible to keep a tomcat as a pet in a city apartment, since it is too difficult for the mature male cat to remain housebroken if he is kept indoors. Altering a male cat sometimes brings about unexpected results; occasionally it causes a cat to become fat and lazy; but in Albert's case he simply grew up to be—as far as I could judge—a cheerful perennial adolescent as far as sex was concerned.

The Bruiser might have killed Albert, I suppose, if Albert had been a straightforward tomcat. As it was the two of them fought some fairly violent fights. But the fights always stopped in time. And Albert, meanwhile, seemed to be receiving lessons from the Bruiser in how to fight back. The Bruiser had a wicked right hook. If he cut Albert's ear, it was always Albert's left ear. Presently, with mixed emotions, I realized that Albert had developed his own right hook; when the Bruiser went by our window, I saw that he had acquired a few fresh nicks on his own left ear.

The Bruiser dominated the roof below us for the first three or four years of Albert's life. During spring and summer the fights he kicked up—with other cats as well as with Albert—were lively and frequent. But during the winter he was

not so spry. Presently in cold weather he would come and sit on our windowsill and gaze in through the glass. But on those cold days he did not stare brashly at Albert, challenging him to a glaring match. He simply looked in with a lost and agonized look, as though he wondered at a world or a God that could cause him to suffer so much. His feet would be cracked and cut from the snow; the patches of mange on his back, becoming more widespread as time went by, would look raw and inflamed from the cold; and when he moved he would move stiffly, as though suffering from rheumatism. Even though he was Albert's archenemy I sometimes tried to invite him indoors, but he never would come. The best I could do was to leave food for him outside the window. Albert himself appeared to approve of this. The Bruiser would limp hastily away when I opened the window, but when the window was closed he would come back and bolt down the food.

Little by little he grew less afraid of me, and in the fourth winter he gained enough confidence to accept an occasional piece of food from my fingers. But then in February of that year he disappeared, and I never saw him again.

Albert had already wrested control of the roof from the Bruiser during the preceding year. From that time forward no other cat ever succeeded in challenging his right to dominate the backyard area. Albert had, it seems, inherited it from the Bruiser; the crown prince had succeeded to his kingship.

Occasionally he had to work hard to maintain his authority. And occasionally I worried about him. There were times when he returned home rumpled and exhausted. Every so often he would suffer a bite that became infected, and we would have to go visit Dr. S., the local veterinarian. Dr. S. was a nice brisk young man who wore Murray Space Shoes. He would study Albert's latest wound and sigh exasperatedly. He took a dim view of Albert's mode of living. "Why don't you keep him indoors?" he would ask. I found it impossible to give him any succinct answer. How to explain, in the first place, that Albert would not let me keep him indoors, and, in the second place, that Albert would cease to be Albert if I tried to limit his life to one small narrow apartment?

I took to worrying double-time, however, when four large French poodles moved into one of Albert's favorite gardens on Waverly Place.

It was a large and elegant garden, and it appeared to belong to a large and elegant duplex apartment. Presumably the poodles' owners were the new tenants of the apartment. But Albert, it seemed, had no respect whatsoever for the rights of such as tenants. He cared not one whit that, according to law, those large black standard-sized poodles had every right to be in that garden, and that he had none. He claimed squatters' rights. It had been his garden for years. Why should the poodles take it over? I saw him studying the situation from the roof below my window, and he looked miffed and angry.

Soon after that he invented a game of sitting on the poodles' fence. The fence was about eight feet high, and Albert, crouched securely on top of it, would dangle his tail just above he noses of the poodles. The poodles naturally were infuriated. Ancient Gallic honor was insulted; ancient Gallic blood was roused. Leaping, barking, filled with rage, the poodles would exhaust themselves trying to get hold of Albert's tail. But if they ever came really close to that appendage, Albert would flick the tip of it neatly out of their reach.

At first, when the poodles barked, I would run nervously to my window to look out. But gradually I came to know their voices, and I understood that their frenzied barking signified only frustration. Subconsciously I began to wait for a different note to enter their voices before I took real alarm.

Then one day I heard what I had feared to hear—an enormous, overpowering roar of canine excitement, the roar of dogs who have cornered their quarry.

In panic, I rushed to the window, but it was all over before I got there. The barks had changed to yelps of anguish, and an incredible tableau met my eyes. In the middle of the elegant garden Albert was standing calmly, not even fluffed out, with his right paw raised in a position of right-hook readiness. In the four corners of the garden, screaming fearfully, cowered the four French poodles.

I do not know how Albert had gotten into that exact situation; perhaps he had entered the garden while the poodles were in the house, and had been caught there. At any rate he stood in the center in calm command. But how long he could retain that command I was not certain. An alarmed woman had already rushed out of the duplex apartment and was coming to the aid of the poodles.

Without taking time to think about it, spontaneously, worriedly, I leaned out of my remote and lofty window and called Albert's name.

It still astonishes me to remember that Albert heard and obeyed me. Or perhaps it was simply that my summons fitted in with is own plans. Anyway he turned slowly, gave the poodles one last lordly look, went to the fence, leaped up it, and returned to my window at a deliberate pace.

I must admit that I felt proud of him. "Well, Albert," I said, "I guess you won that round, didn't you?"

He smugly accepted a pat, sat down on the windowsill, and licked his whiskers. And then—I may have imagined it, but it does seem to me that it actually happened—he looked down at his tail, and with supreme self-satisfaction he moved the end of it in one delicate, expertly controlled twitch.

* * *

That was the way it was with him in the outside world of Greenwich Village. Indoors, however, he often dropped his regal pose. If for instance he wanted food, he was capable of acting and looking as helpless as any orphan kitten. He put on this act for my neighbors, too, and for quite a while the neighbors—people who lived above me and below me off the fire escape—took to feeding him because they thought he had no home. Eventually I met these people in the hallway of the building, and we identified each other and compared notes. "I thought he was getting rather fat for a stray," said one neighbor. Another neighbor, a nice lady who worked for a magazine, confessed that sometimes she even fed Albert caviar. She told me he liked it, too.

So it is that when I see Albert now, in my mind's eye, I see him in a variety of contradictory attitudes. I not only see him walking royally along the back fences of his kingdom; I also see him standing by my icebox, with that orphan-kitten look, giving a piteous mew as he tells me it is time for dinner; or I see him sprawled at his gray-striped ease on the studio couch, with his front paws spread wide, lying lionlike, large-chested; or I see him sitting like a witch's familiar on my mantelpiece, regarding me through those enormous, hypnotic, lime-green eyes; or I see him curled in my lap, purring, stretching up his chin for a scratch;

or I see him darting with abandon after a ping-pong ball, or growing marvelously drunk while he indulges in an orgy of catnip mice; or I see him tunneling under a blanket thrown down for play and emerging rumpled, raffish, tail lashing, from the other side; or I see him stretching his muscles upward as he sharpens his claws on the easy chair, giving me meanwhile that I-dare-you-to-stop-me look.

I owned him for a full nine years, and then circumstances forced me to give him away. I had to move to another apartment, and the apartment shortage in New York was such that I was unable to find an apartment that would give Albert access to the outdoors. Penned inside at last, he was so miserable that he cried at the window all day and all night, and there was no solution except to find him a better home. Fortunately he had three devoted friends in Massachusetts, three single ladies, sisters, the aunts of a good friend of mine. With them Albert had already spent several summer vacations, working for his keep defending their vegetable garden against predator rabbits. These three friends were eager to offer Albert a year-round establishment where he could get in and out as much as he pleased.

I let him go to them with as little fanfare as I could, knowing that he would be happier with them than with me. It was a hard decision to make, and there is no sense dwelling on the wrench that I felt. But I soon had the consolation of knowing that he was happy in his new home. His friends teach music in a small New England city, and Albert always liked music, especially classical music. Now while one of his present owners gives singing lessons, he sits on the piano and listens. If any student sings a note off-key, he glares appropriately. Or that, I am told, is what the students think he does.

This then is a reminiscence about an animal that does not end with his death, but with the time when he parted company with his first owner.

I have not seen him in seven years—I avoided seeing him after I gave him away—but I am surprised still at how much he meant and still means to me, at how deeply a seemingly casual relationship with a pet animal can become part of one's life, can shape and change one's attitudes. I first acquired Albert, really, only for amusement, but he demanded something more of me, something honorable, something more respectful of the manifestations of life. I suppose that an animal

by his very existence challenges an owner to understand him, and the better one understands the animal the better one understands oneself, or certain aspects of oneself. Touch an animal, and often, surprisingly, you find that you touch your own psyche. Touch an animal, and sometimes, by an odd kind of grace, you touch the source of life.

Animals acquire all sorts of symbolic overtones for their owners, and perhaps Albert, part and parcel of my youth, of the years when I was in my twenties, acquired even extra overtones for me; he was so fine a symbol of the youthful soul, sometimes daring, sometimes terrified, sometimes infantile, but almost always brash, going forth into the complex world to seek, with high hopes, knowledge and fulfillment. He has gone on now to another phase of his life even as I have.

I like to picture him in Massachusetts, pampered by his three present owners, keeping their singing students in line. But I have a feeling that he runs still through the alleys of the night back on Eighth Street—not just at times, but for always. It is perhaps four o'clock in the morning, and he has been out prowling for some two hours, and he slips again like a shadow past a dark cellar way, up a fence, down into one yard, then over into another; then into the poodles' deserted garden; then up their fence and along the top of it to his own special roof. On the roof he pauses and looks about and sniffs the air that is freshening with dawn. He is tired now, and all is well in his kingdom. So he walks slowly to the fire escape, and up, one flight, two flights, to his own open window, even as the dawn begins to brighten in the sky. Once through the window, he crosses the room and jumps up onto my old studio couch, and I, a younger woman than I am now, murmur in my sleep, turn, touch him, and sleep again. For an old life may change to a new one, but the old life remains in the new. A new day may come; but love endures, and that which we love, even a cat, even an animal, that which we love is for always.

* * * *

"Albert," by Blythe Morley Brennan. Included in Animal Stories *(New York: Dell Publishing Co., 1965). If anyone can provide knowledge of the author or heirs of the author, please relay this information to Joe Wheeler (P.O. Box 1246, Conifer, CO 80433). Blythe Morley Brennan wrote for the popular press during the first half of the twentieth century.*

THE KINGLY CAT

-Dee Dunsing-

Rachel needed a live cat for a model. But when she finally found one, he refused to cooperate.
What should she do?

* * *

Rachel Harwood got up early one frosty Saturday morning in November and, after breakfast, hurried out to her study over the garage. There she adjusted the curtains to let in as much of the winter sunlight as possible and sat down before a large sheet of drawing paper.

"I'll do a cat," she murmured thoughtfully, as she picked up a stick of charcoal. "What is more graceful than a cat—an indolent one, lying in the sun?"

She had no model except the humpy, mad-looking cat that adorned the bookends on her table; but she hopefully looked at him with the idea of getting proper proportions. In a few moments she began to sketch.

But her work didn't go well. By ten o'clock when the twinkling-eyed Scott Timmons, who lived next door, came tramping in to see where she was keeping herself, she was thoroughly discouraged.

"I can't do it, Scott," she explained dismally, as he sat down in her best chair and draped his feet across the arm. "And I especially wanted to, because the best ones are to be exhibited in Indianapolis."

"Well, try again," urged Scott. "You're not one of those wobbly, sink-down, give-up folks, I hope."

"I simply can't do it without a living model."

"A cat should be easy to get," observed Scott, to whom obstacles were the breath of life. "Shep's always chasing them out of our yard."

"But it's winter now, and they're all inside of houses," Rachel pointed out. "I haven't seen a cat for weeks."

Scott shrugged. "Then you'd better draw something else, or be in the flower booth."

Rachel was silent for a moment. Then she said softly, "Scott, you've heard me thumping on the piano for years, haven't you?"

"I'll say," agreed Scott heartily, "and do you thump! It sounds like a milk wagon getting run into."

"Well, I've endured your cornet long enough to make up for anything you've suffered," retorted Rachel. "But that's not the point. The point is that I'm afraid Aunt Bertha won't let me stop music and begin art until I prove that I have real artistic ability. Now do you see?"

"I begin to, dimly," acknowledged Scott.

"And if I can't enter a drawing and get a prize, I'll have to give myself up to thump-thumping for goodness knows how long."

"Enough," said Scott, rising to his feet. "I shall fetch you a cat." After which he made a fantastic flourish with his hands as if he were doffing a plumed hat, called "Farewell!" and backed out the study door.

In three-quarters of an hour he was back with a triumphant grin on his face and a draggled bundle of black fur under his arm.

"Mademoiselle, your cat," he announced proudly as he set the creature on the floor.

Rachel stared at it. Never in all her life had she seen a cat like this. It was green-eyed and dirty and thin and full of complaining, hungry meows; but overshadowing all these characteristics was a V-shaped white stripe down the middle of its back, which made it look startlingly like a skunk.

"Are you sure it's a cat?" Rachel asked uncertainly.

"I wondered about that myself," admitted Scott, "but it passes all the cat tests."

"Let's give it some food and a bath," said Rachel impulsively. "Then maybe it'll stretch out in the sun and go to sleep. That's what I want—an indolent cat, so I can draw him that way."

Scott assisted with the feeding and washing, and in no time the cat was purring contentedly and his straggly fur looked clean and fluffy. Rachel put him in the sun and asked him to lie down and look indolent, but he refused. He preferred to sit straight, with a haughty air that was so unmistakably regal that Scott insisted on naming him Nero.

"It's lunch time now," observed Rachel, glancing at her wristwatch, "but after lunch I'm going to start work. And with a real live model, I'll do a sketch that'll make old Shep bark himself hoarse."

"Good luck to you," Scott replied.

* * *

The following Wednesday when Scott dropped in after school, he found Rachel's drawing making a big bulge in the wastepaper basket and Rachel looking as if she had cried herself completely tearless.

"And what," he asked, with a solicitous frown, "is the matter? It looked dandy when you showed it to me the other night."

"It was hopeless," said Rachel dully, "so I wadded it up and threw it away. It didn't have any life or any indolence. It was no good."

Scott picked up the crumpled paper and straightened it. For a long moment he gazed at the charcoal drawing. Then he too wadded it up and threw it in the basket. "You're right," he agreed. "It's not good at all. Not nearly up to what you've done before. Why couldn't you make it go?"

Rachel glanced toward where Nero sat regally in the leather chair as if it were his throne. His green eyes were wide and shiny, his front legs were rigidly straight,

his whole attitude was as kingly as if he ruled the entire city. Even the white stripe down his back, the stripe that usually made him look like a skunk, appeared now to be a narrow, ermine-edged cape hanging from his shoulders.

"It's that cat," she said with certainty. "He sits there all day long just like that. When I try to make him lie down and look indolent, he struggles and gets up immediately. I can't do a thing with him."

Scott surveyed the cat thoughtfully. "That's funny. Cats aren't usually like that. Doesn't he ever sleep?"

"I've never seen him sleep. All he does is chew my dictionary," said Rachel, holding out a book with a gnawed backbone. "I've spanked him, but he won't stop chewing it."

"I see," mused Scott. "He sits like a king on a throne or else he tries to eat the dictionary. Poor fellow, I'm afraid he's trying to act like Alexander the Great instead of just a plain cat who looks like a skunk. Can't say I blame him."

"Whatever he's doing," complained Rachel, "it's keeping me from drawing an indolent cat."

"But he can't be indolent," objected Scott. "Don't you see? It would upset his dignity. You'll just have to draw him as he is."

"Draw him as he is?" repeated Rachel.

At first the idea seemed absurd to her. Start over now, just when she had cried her eyes out because of her other failure? Try drawing the same cat, when she had made a fizzle of him once? But the more she gazed at Nero's regal magnificence, at the stern grace of neck and limb, the more impressed she became. He was lovely in that pose, and he held it by the hour. All she would have to do was copy.

"Come on, Rachel," urged Scott. "Try it again. I know you can win a prize."

Slowly Rachel got out another piece of drawing paper. "All right, Scott," she agreed. "I'll try just once more."

* * *

A week later at ten o'clock one night she finished the sketch. She had sat up late to do it, afire with enthusiasm and dazzled with her prospect of success.

When the last shadow had been added, she set the picture on her desk and stood off a way to survey it. Yes, it was good. Just as good as she had hoped, and possibly better. It surpassed anything she had ever done.

She was so tired and yet so excited that she trembled all over. Surely this picture couldn't escape winning a prize. Surely it would be sent to the exhibit at Indianapolis.

It seemed as if that whole night, from the moment she turned out the light and got into bed until Aunt Bertha woke her in the morning, was only a wink in time. She was still enchanted with the memory of her sketch, still hardly able to believe that she had done anything so fine. In a trance she dressed and ate breakfast. But before she started to school, she wanted one more look at her masterpiece.

Nero was up when she opened the door, only this morning he was half-lying, washing his black coat with his pink tongue.

"Hi, there, Nero," Rachel cried happily, feeling a deep affection for the cat who had helped her do her picture so beautifully. She turned toward the desk, expecting to see the charcoal sketch proudly displayed as she had left it the night before.

It was there, but not as she had left it. It lay on the desk, one corner of it folded back by the toppled-over dictionary, which looked more chewed than ever. The ink bottle had been upset, and half its contents made a black pool across the body of the charcoal cat. Several inky cat footprints smudged the unblotted portion.

With a cry, Rachel ran toward it, released it from the book, and poured off the pool of ink. But that didn't improve it much. It was unalterably spoiled, ruined beyond repair.

She turned on Nero, ready to shower him with reproaches. But he had stopped licking his fur and was looking at her with a faint sheepishness as if he were utterly wretched and miserable inside. He knew it had been a bad thing to do. Not at all kingly. And he was ashamed.

Rachel dashed the tears out of her eyes and ran downstairs and out into the brisk, cold morning. It was late, and she would have to hurry. A block ahead of her she saw Scott, but she didn't call to him. She didn't want to talk to anyone.

Only when Scott dropped the book he was trying to balance on top of his head did he notice her. Then he waited while Rachel caught up. "The cat ruined my drawing," she said at once, knowing that she would have to tell him sooner or later. "He spilled ink on it."

Scott was sympathetic. "Say, that's tough. How'd it happen?"

She explained, and Scott shook his head. "Poor old Nero," he observed. "He was trying to be intellectual, and he balled things all up."

"Well, I wish he'd try being some other cat," remarked Rachel bitterly. "Or I wish I'd never seen him at all."

"Now, now," Scott soothed, "Nero made a wonderful model for your second drawing. Don't be down on him. Give him another chance."

"I couldn't do another picture," said Rachel gloomily. "Even if I felt like it, there wouldn't be enough time. The sketches go on exhibit tomorrow evening."

"There's one more chance to use Nero at the school fair," said Scott. "Of course it won't be nearly as nice as having a picture in the art exhibit or getting a sketch sent to Indianapolis, but it would be something if Nero won a prize in the pet show, wouldn't it?"

"Well," agreed Rachel slowly, "it wouldn't help me with my particular problem, but it would be better than nothing. Only how—with that funny stripe . . ."

"You'd have to enter him under the 'Pets With Character' division," Scott told her.

* * *

The high school was abuzz with people and excitement. In the gym, where the pet show was going on, ribbons had just been awarded to fond owners of prize-winning animals. In a booth labeled "Pets With Character," Rachel stood proudly behind a table where sat Nero. In spite of the noise and excitement, Nero preserved his dignity, as if he knew what the blue ribbon on his collar meant. Only his wide green eyes and the occasional flicker of an ear betrayed his tenseness.

"Did you ever see such a cat!" people had been gasping all evening. And then they would say, "Why he . . . he looks like a king or like a president!" Most people said "king," and several remarked that his V-stripe looked like ermine trimming on a black robe. Nobody mentioned a skunk—not because they were too polite, but because they didn't think of it.

He's acting like a king, thought Rachel, *and so people see him that way. Maybe Scott and I wouldn't even have thought of skunks if Nero hadn't been so miserable and skulking that first morning.* While she greeted people and told them how she had got Nero, the thought kept working around in the back of her brain. Finally it came around to herself. *If I should act like an artist, maybe people would accept me as one, and Aunt Bertha would let me give up my music.* But that was a little hard to believe, because Rachel felt that she had been acting like an artist, and nothing had come of it.

Someone tweaked her elbow, and she turned to find Scott grinning down at her. "Girl, I've got the best news you ever heard."

"What?" gasped Rachel.

"I met your Aunt Bertha out in the corridor. While I was talking to her I mentioned that you wanted to be an artist. She threw her hands up in the air and said, 'Oh, my goodness, don't I know it? What else could I think when she draws all day and all night? She really does wonderfully, too. I'm going to get her a teacher.' "

"A teacher!" echoed Rachel, all atremble with delight. "Did she honestly, Scott? You're not fooling me, are you?"

"I am not," replied Scott. "And that's not all. I said, 'Well, Mrs. Brown, it's about time you put a stop to that awful thumpety-thumping that Rachel's been doing over there. It's nearly driven me mad.' And do you know what she said? She shrieked with laughter, then leaned over and patted me on the shoulder and said, 'Poor boy, I sympathize with you. It's nearly driven me into a decline. But if Rachel takes up art, she won't be interested in music anymore.' "

"Oh, Scott," breathed Rachel. "It's all so grand I can't think of what to say or do."

"You owe a lot to your Uncle Scott," he said severely, "and you've got to pay him back. Right now he wants to treat you to ice cream and cookies in the domestic science room. Come on."

* * * * *

"The Kingly Cat," by Dee Dunsing. Published November 8, 1936, in The Girl's Companion. *Reprinted by permission of Joe Wheeler (P.O. Box 1246, Conifer, CO 80433) and Cook Communications Ministries, Colorado Springs, CO. Dee Dunsing wrote for popular and inspirational magazines during the first half of the twentieth century.*

PANDORA'S BOOKS

-Joseph Leininger Wheeler-

It was just an old bookstore, wasn't it?
She found it to be far more than that . . . and Pandora was a cat!

* * *

PROLOGUE

Later it would be remembered as "the year with no spring." All the more surprising because it had been a bitterly cold winter, complete with record snowfall, frequent ice storms, traffic gridlock on the Washington D.C. Beltway, closed airports, and snow days—longed for by children and teachers alike.

At first, people assumed it to be a fluke—*surely* the geese couldn't possibly be flying north already! Why the iced-over Potomac and Severn Rivers were only now beginning to break up. But the honking geese kept coming, attuned to their planet's moods in ways humans will never understand.

Surely the cherry blossoms down on the Tidal Basin couldn't possibly be blooming this early! And the daffodils too? . . . . But they were—and those who delayed but a day missed Jefferson's lagoon at its loveliest, for unseasonably

warm air, coupled with sudden wind, stripped the blossoms from the unbeliev-
ing trees.

Azaleas and dogwood were next—way too early, as well. Usually, the multi-
hued azalea, along with dogwood of pink and white, ravished the senses for weeks
every spring. Not so this year; they came and went in only days. By early April,
the thermometer had already climbed to a hundred, and schools began to close
now because of the heat instead of the cold.

Once entrenched, the heat dug in, and the mercury kept climbing. Even the
spring rains failed to come, and farmers shook their heads, trembling in their mort-
gages.

Plants dried up; lawns turned brown in spite of frequent watering; and
centuries-old trees dropped their already-yellowish leaves in abject defeat.

Tourists stayed home, making sizzling Washington a veritable ghost town; for
the first time in recent memory, one could park anywhere—no waiting, no endless circling.

And for those Washingtonians who did not have air-conditioning in home,
office, and cars, it was awful. One couldn't even escape by boat, for prolonged
calms plagued the Chesapeake, interspersed by blasting gales of fierce, tinder-dry
winds.

On TV weather maps, the entire eastern seaboard turned brown in early
April—and stayed brown, altering only to a *deeper* hue of brown. There was sort
of a morbid fascination in watching as heat record after heat record fell before
that immovable front, seemingly set in concrete.

So . . . when the weather reporters trumpeted the glad news that, come
Memorial Day weekend, the siege would at last be lifted and blessed coolness
from Canada would flow in, most people greeted it as a second Armistice Day, a
time to climb out of their bunkers and celebrate.

Traffic jams clogged roads everywhere, and Highway 50 became a parking
lot from Washington to Ocean City. Strangely enough, the euphoria ran so high
that people didn't seem to mind; they got out of their cars and vans, set up their
lawn chairs on the median, threw frisbees back and forth, and ate picnic lunches.
One enterprising caravan of college students found enough room between their

cars to play a screwy sort of volleyball in the middle of the Chesapeake Bay Bridge!

But some people find happiness in places other than the beach. Places like bookstores. Used bookstores. Pandora's bookstore.

* * *

Oh, it feels so great to have a cool day again! mused Jennifer as she drove onto Highway 50 with the top down for the first time in—well, it *seemed* a year. It felt good just to let her hair fly loose in the wind. As Annapolis loomed ahead, she veered off on Riva Road and then headed south on Highway 2. Stick-um'd to her checkbook were Amy's directions.

"Oh Jen, you'll just *love* it," her closest friend had raved. "It's unlike any other bookstore you've ever seen!"

Jennifer, a veteran of hundreds of used bookstores, strongly doubted that, but not wanting to flatly contradict her friend, she merely mumbled a muffled, "Oh?"

Amy, noting the doubt written on her face—Jennifer never *had* been able to keep a secret, for her expressive face gave it away every time—merely grinned and looked wise. "Jus' you wyte, 'En'ry Iggens, jus' you wyte!" she caroled.

In the intervening weeks and months since that challenge, several other friends had rhapsodized about this one-of-a-kind bookstore, each report racheting Jennifer's curiosity up another notch.

Now, on this absolutely perfect late May day, she saw no reason to delay further. She would see this hyped-way-beyond-its-worth place herself. After all, there were no other claims on her day . . . *more's the pity,* she told herself. And her truant memory wafted her backwards without ever asking permission—backwards to a time when she *had* been needed, *had* been wanted, *had* been loved. *Or . . . ,* she qualified to herself, *at least I* thought *he loved me!*

It had been one of those childhood romances adults so often chuckle about. The proverbial boy next door. They had played together day by day—inside one of their homes in bad weather; outside the rest of the time. When school started, they entered first grade together.

He carried her books, fought anyone who mistreated her, and at home they studied together.

He had been the first boy to hold her hand, the first she had kissed. Their parents had merely laughed in that condescending way adults have about young love, and prophesied, "Puppy love *never* lasts. Just watch! They'll find someone else."

But they didn't find "somebody else." Not even when puberty messed them up inside, recontoured their bodies, redirected their thoughts. Each remained the other's all.

They even chose the same college—and studied together still. Went to concerts and art galleries together, hiked the mountains together, walked—barefoot—the beaches together, haunted bookstores together, went to parties together, even attended church together.

So it had come as no surprise that spring break of their senior year when, walking among the dunes near Cape Hatteras, he asked her to marry him. And there was no hesitation in her joyous, "Yes, Bill."

That it somehow lacked passion, that there was little yearning for the other physically, didn't seem to matter. Hadn't their relationship stood the test of time? How much longer than twenty years would it take to *know*, for goodness sake!

So the date had been set, the wedding party chosen, the bridal and attendants' dresses made, the flowers ordered, the tuxes measured, the minister and chapel secured, the honeymoon destination booked, the apartment they would live in arranged for, the wedding invitations sent out.

And then—thirty-six hours before the wedding—her world had caved in on her. Bill had come over and asked if they could talk. "Of course!" she had smiled, chalking up the tense look on his face to groom-jitters.

They sat down in their favorite swing on the back porch and looked out at the yard, already festive for the reception to be held there. Her smile faded quickly as she took in his haggard face, the eyes with dark circles around them. Premonition froze her into glacial immobility. Surely it couldn't be what she, deep down, sensed it would be. Not after all these years!

But it was. He could only stammer brokenly the chopped up words and phrases that amputated two dreams that over a twenty-year period had grown within hours of becoming one. He had found someone whose presence—or absence—raised him to the skies or plunged him to the depths, someone who ignited his hormones to such an extent that life without her was unthinkable. Bill hadn't gone far before his face turned scarlet and he began to sputter.

In mercy, Jennifer broke in: "Don't say anything more, Bill," she cried in a strangely ragged voice. "You can't force love—not the real, lifetime kind. I . . . I'd far rather know this now than later." She paused for control.

Bill could only sit there miserably, his head in his hands.

So it was up to her to finish this thing. She knew she would always love him; after all, he had been her best friend for almost as far back as she could remember. And there is no trap door to open and dump such things—for the memories remain *always* and cannot be so easily disposed of.

He couldn't bring himself to face her parents, so after a few more minutes they stood up; there was one last hug—and he walked away.

She salvaged a bit of her battered pride by calling off the wedding herself. That was the hardest thing she had ever done. Numbly, she phoned them all, but gave no reasons. They would know why soon enough, if they didn't know already.

And so her marital dreams had died.

A year passed, and another, and another . . . until six years separated her from that fateful parting that, like "no man's land," separated the girl from the woman—trust and unconditional acceptance on the one side from suspicion and reserve on the other.

During the first two years, she had turned down all the men who asked her out. But, gradually, as her bludgeoned self-esteem began to get up off the floor, she belatedly realized that life must go on, that she must not wall herself off from living. So she began to date again, but not very often. Nine months of the year the children in her third-grade classroom were her world. During the other three she took graduate work, traveled, wrote, visited art galleries, attended plays, concerts, and operas. Often alone, but frequently with dear friends such as Amy, or with her brother James.

She sometimes wondered if she would ever find the kind of mate Bill had found—the kind of magnetism that would call her even across the proverbial "crowded room." Would there ever be someone who would set her heart singing? Who would be the friend Bill had been, but who would also arouse a passionate yearning to be his physical, mental, social, and spiritual mate? Every once in a while, she would wonder, *Why is it so difficult to find the one? Is there something wrong with me?*

So the long hours, days, weeks, months, and years passed. She completed her master's at Johns Hopkins, and she was invariably doing *something*, anything, to avoid admitting to herself that she was unutterably lonely.

None of her diversions worked.

Not one.

* * *

Oh, she had almost missed her road! She slammed on the brakes, almost getting rear-ended in the process, and turned left. "Three and seven-tenths miles," Amy had said. Sure enough, there loomed the sign: "PANDORA'S BOOKS."

Gotta be a story here somewhere, she smiled. Now she slowed and turned into an ancient-looking brick gateway. A couple of hundred feet inside was another sign announcing that this was a wildlife sanctuary. *Some bookstore!*

The road snaked its way through first-growth trees (according to report, one of the only such stands of timber left on this part of the Chesapeake). Here and there azalea, rhododendron, and wild laurel bushes banked the road.

She slowed the Camaro to a crawl, to give some deer time to get off the road. Birds seemed to be everywhere—cardinals, goldfinches, sparrows, even a couple of bluebirds—and high overhead, hawks and gulls. It seemed incongruous to discover such solitude this close to the Washington metroplex of six million people.

At last the road straightened out and dropped down into the strangest parking lot she had ever seen. Following directions from a sign, she drove into another grove of trees until she came to a pull-in without a vehicle in it. After putting the top up and locking the car, she found a path to the beach.

She sensed the water's edge before she could see it, and now she could plainly hear the *ca-ca-ca-ca* of the gulls. Suddenly, there it was: blinding white clapboard, framed by the silver-flecked blue of the Chesapeake. No clouds overhead today, only seagulls, and on the water, like swans taking flight, sailboats . . . as far as the eye could see. She stopped, transfixed, and inwardly spoke these words to her best Friend: *Lord, thank You for this day—this almost-too-beautiful-to-be-true day.*

She had always been more intense than any of her acquaintances, and more deeply affected by beauty.

Before going in, she added a rather strange postscript: *Lord, please let only good things happen to me today.* Then she opened the door and walked in.

Inside, classical music was playing softly, meshing wondrously with the lapping of the waves on the shore, the cry of the gulls, and the occasional raucous croak that could come only from the long throat of a great blue heron.

And ah, that one-of-a-kind fragrance of old books, which to book-lovers is the true wine of life! And not marred, as is sadly true of so many used bookstores, with disorganization, overstocking, clutter, and grime. She set out to analyze why.

First of all, it was clean—not antiseptically so, but just close enough. No grime besmirched the shelves, books, walls, windows, or the floor. Second, although the store contained tens of thousands of books, there was no perception of clutter or of being engulfed by the sheer mass of it all. It was easy to see why— masses of books were broken up by old prints, paintings, sculpture, bric-a-brac, and flowers. *Real* flowers. She could tell that by their fragrance! And the windows—*open* windows, today—to let in the outside world. Or just enough of it. And there were benches and soft chairs everywhere, graced by lamps of great beauty.

Quickly, she discovered that the artwork tied in perfectly with the genre displayed on the shelves. For instance, Remingtons and Russells dominated the walls of the western room, supplemented by dust jacket originals, magazine art, movie posters, lobby cards, and old photographs. The adolescent/youth section had as its focal center a wondrous display of Maxfield Parrish, with its pièce de résistance, the largest print she'd ever seen of his *Ecstasy*. Blow-ups of dust jackets, paperbacks, and magazine art graced the walls in just the right places.

And amazingly, different music played in every room. Softly. In the western room could be heard most of the old standard western artists, from The Sons of the Pioneers to Eddy Arnold. In the religion and philosophy room, she heard the great music of the church. Lilting, happy music flowed from the children's room.

But best of all was the literature and general fiction room. For one thing, it dominated the seaward side of the second story. And on walls where no direct sunlight would fade what hung there, she saw faithfully reproduced copies of old masters: Zurbarán, Titian, Leonardo, Ribera, Caravaggio, La Tour, and Rembrandt.

A massive stone fireplace anchored the southeastern corner. Just to its right stood a nine-foot grand piano. On its shiny surface was flopped in abandoned comfort as beautiful a Himalayan as Jennifer had ever seen. Without even thinking, she crossed the room toward it and reached out her hand, allowing it to be sniffed before she ventured to scratch the cat's head and massage its ears. A loud purring told her that she had been accepted into the narrow circle that could induce purring.

Jennifer crossed to one of the open windows, leaned against the sill, and gazed out across the silver-flecked blue. Then—ever so softly, floating out of the very walls it seemed—she heard those haunting first bars of Chopin's *Étude in E*. It was just too much; her intensely passionate nature could handle only so much circuit overload. She lost all track of time or reality.

* * *

Coming up the stairs with a load of books for restocking, Arthur sighed. On this seemingly perfect day he longed to be outside. But so did his employees, so he had let many of them go. Reluctantly. As he heard *Étude in E,* he slowed his pace. No matter how often he heard it, that *Étude* got him every time. Something in its melody brought an ache, reminded him that he was alone—incomplete. Thus his normal defenses melted like wax when he stepped into the room which housed his classics—and stopped, rooted to the floor, when he saw the figure

staring out the window. Her sapphire blue dress draped long, loose, and Maxfield Parrish classical; her complexion cameo ivory; her long hair a copperish flame; her ankles and Teva-sandled feet slim and graceful. A pre-Raphaelite painting suddenly come to life there in the room. He hardly dared breathe lest he break her trance.

Subconsciously, he weighed the external pieces that added up to the totality. *No,* he concluded, *she is not beautiful, though she has classical features and classical form, but she's alive, as alive as any woman I have ever seen.* He watched, as the strains of *Étude in E* internalized in her heart and soul and overflowed into her face—that face which always mirrored her inner self in spite of all efforts to control it. A tear glistened in an eye, the color of which he could not from that angle see, and slowly made a pathway down her cheek. But in her reverie she did not even notice it. Strangely enough, even though he'd never seen her before, he yearned to wipe that tear away and find out what caused it—if it was the *Étude* . . . or if it was something more.

* * *

Something woke her, told her she was no longer alone. She turned slightly and saw him standing there, photographing her with his blue-gray eyes. (Hers, he now discovered, were an amazingly burnished emerald green.) Gradually, as the mists of her trance dissipated, he came into full focus. He stood 6' 2", dark brown hair salted with premature gray, trim, physically fit. Dressed well, in a button-up chambray shirt, khaki Dockers, and slip-on loafers. Probably in mid- to late-thirties.

But his face . . . she felt instinctively that this man standing there knew pain, for it etched his face. Especially did she note it in the ever-so-slight droop of a mouth that seemed made for smiling. His eyes, she concluded, were wonderfully kind. (He was not photographing her with pin-up intentions, but with tenderness and concern, and for such ammunition, she had no defense. Until that moment, she had never needed any.)

Feeling a familiar softness rubbing against his leg, he looked down and smiled. She liked that smile . . . and wished to prolong its stay. Clearing her throat, she spoke just one word, "Yours?"

And his smile grew broader as he tenderly picked up the purring cat, cradled it in his muscular arms, and announced, "Pandora."

She laughed, a delightfully throaty laugh, and retorted, "So here is the real owner of all these books!"

He laughed too. "Yes, well it's a long story. If you're not in a hurry, I'll tell you."

I'm not in a hurry, she decided. *Never in less of one in all my life.*

So they sat down on opposite ends of a sofa, and he told her the saga of a Himalayan kitten who was into *everything* (hence her name)! and how she had wrapped her tiny little soul around his when things weren't going very well for him (and Jennifer sensed that admittance to be a major understatement). So when certain developments made possible this bookstore, in gratitude, he had named it in her honor.

And he smiled again. "It *is* her bookstore. I'm sure she feels it is hers, perhaps more so than a human ever could. And our customers . . . well, the people who come here feel she is boss. Everyone asks about her, and no one ever wants to leave without paying his or her respects." He chuckled again, "I'm not so important; not many feel short-changed if they leave without seeing me."

She thought, but did not say, *I'm afraid—I'm very afraid—that I would.*

So interested did she become in the story of this wonderfully different bookstore that she kept at him until the entire story spilled out. Even, or perhaps *especially,* a brief account of the motivation for it—the failure of a relationship central in his life. He did not elaborate.

Other book-lovers came and went, eyed the man, woman, and dozing cat on the couch, attempted to listen in, and reluctantly moved on. Three times, they suffered interruptions—once for a customer downstairs, once for a phone call, and once by refreshments brought up by the assistant manager. Noticing her raised eyebrows, he explained that fresh-brewed coffee (regular and decaf) and herbal tea was always ready on both floors, as were bagels and cookies, cold sodas, and bottles of fruit juice.

"Yeah," he admitted, coffee's one of my many besetting sins . . . the jump start that gets me going. Maybe it isn't very smart to mix coffee and snacks with books . . . but real book lovers rarely mistreat books. No one's wrecked a book yet

because of it! But no smoking! I can't stand it, and . . ." he looked down at the sleeping cat on his lap, "neither can Pandora."

Suddenly, Jennifer looked at her watch and jumped to her feet: "I can't believe it. Where has the day gone? So sorry . . . but I gotta' run. Thanks ever so much for everything, but I'm late for an appointment. But I'll be back! Bye-bye, Pandora." And she stopped to give the cat one last scratch under the chin. Then she was gone, without so much as revealing her name.

But then, he mused, *neither did I!*

With her departure, although there remained not a cloud in the sky, it seemed to him that a partial eclipse darkened the sun. To Arthur the day had lost its brightness. The droop came back to his lip, but not quite so pronounced as before.

* * *

Jennifer stayed away for almost two weeks, but each day she felt the magnetic pull. Then she'd recoil from her inner yearning to return: *How silly! How ridiculous to blow out of proportion a simple little conversation. He'd probably talk like that to anyone who came by and asked the same questions. After all, he's in the business to make customers and sell books!*

Finally, thoroughly confused by her inner turmoil, she went back—and he wasn't there! But . . . books are books, and she soon lost herself among them. She wanted to ask about him, but could find no reason that didn't seem transparently obvious.

But she did find the books in the vicinity of the check-out stands to be abnormally interesting. She kept taking them off the shelves, one at a time, studying them intently, then returning them to the shelves—all without remembering anything about them! She blushed crimson when it suddenly came to her what she was doing. Scolding herself, *You foolish, foolish schoolgirl, you!* she sheepishly put the last book back on the shelf and moved toward the next room.

She had not waited in vain, however. While she was passing the first cash register, she heard someone ask the clerk where the boss was. She slowed her pace. The clerk's voice was low and pleasing to listen to. "Mr. Bond?" she said.

"Yes, of course! Mr. Bond!"

"Oh . . . uh . . . he didn't tell me where he was going."

Jennifer's sharp ears then picked up a whispered jab from the clerk at the next register: "But you surely wish he had, huh?"

Jennifer sneaked a look. The face of the first speaker flamed scarlet, her blush speaking volumes. *So that's the way the wind blows,* she thought. She appraised the girl carefully: young, at most mid-twenties; statuesque, with midnight black hair (undoubtedly Spanish), and strikingly beautiful.

Even more confused than when she came in, Jennifer hurried out of the bookstore without even looking up Pandora. She was disturbed, angry, and more than a little jealous of this girl who got to work there all the time.

* * *

The three-digit heat returned after the Memorial Day reprieve, and the steamy humidity slowed life to a gasping crawl. Since it was patently too hot outside to do other than wilt like an unwatered impatiens, Jennifer returned again to Pandora's Books.

Looking for him—but not looking for him—she reconnoitered her way through the various rooms, restless as a child the last afternoon of school. Suddenly, she saw him, sitting on an easy chair by the empty fireplace, a portable phone at his ear. And curled around the back of his neck like a fur stole—and just as limp—was Pandora.

Her eyes twinkling, Jennifer surreptitiously edged her way out of the room, assuming he had not seen her. Eventually, she gravitated back to the children's room, in the center of which was a sunken playground; apparently, there were *always* children playing there. After browsing a while, she found a book she had always wanted to read, but could never find—Alcott's *Flower Fables.* Sinking into a soft chair with a seraphic sigh of pure joy, she opened its covers.

But she was not to sink into another world so easily. Across from her, a sandy-haired little boy of about five was vainly trying to capture his mother's attention: "Mama, Mama . . . please, Mama, will you . . ."

"Oh, don't bother me!" she snapped.

Undeterred, the little boy persisted: "But Mama, I found this pretty book, and uh . . . I wonder if you'd . . ."

"Oh, for goodness sake! Will you leave me alone!" she snarled.

At this, the boy recoiled as if struck, and backed away, lips quivering. After one last look at the unyielding face of his mother, engrossed in an Agatha Christie thriller, the child turned and headed toward a raven-haired woman who was restocking books across the room. But his courage wavered as he approached the clerk. Would she rebuff him, too?

By now, Jennifer had forgotten her book completely: *How will the Spanish beauty respond to a child's need?* she asked herself. She didn't have to wait long to find out. The woman, on being tapped on the leg by little fingers, whirled around in surprise. But she did not smile. She had been enduring a raging migraine that afternoon. Milliseconds later, her dark eyes scanned the room to see if anyone had seen. Satisfied that no one had (Jennifer was watching her through veiled eyes, a trick women have and men do not), the clerk brusquely turned her back to the child and continued restocking the shelf.

The little boy didn't cry. He didn't say anything at all. He merely turned around . . . and just stood there, the book still in his hand, lips trembling, and a tear finding its way down his cheek.

It was just too much! Mother or no mother, clerk or no clerk, Jennifer swiftly left her seat and swooped down like a protective hen; then slowed, knelt down, and spoke words kind and gentle, "Can *I* help, dear?" And she tenderly wiped away the tear.

But he had been hurt that afternoon—hurt terribly!—and was no longer as trusting as he had been only minutes before. He just looked at her, eyes *still* puddling. She, respecting his space and his selfhood, didn't touch him again; only waited, with tenderness in her eyes. It was no contest. An instant later, vanquished by those soft eyes, he was in her arms, his eyes wet, his little shoulders heaving, but making not a sound.

Across the room, his mother continued reading.

When the little body had stopped shaking, and the tears had ceased to flow, Jennifer led him to a nearby couch, sat down, and drew him to her. Then she asked him about the book. As he slowly turned the pages and read some of the words, she helped him with the others and explained the illustrations. The look of joy transfigured his face, and excited comprehension filled his voice . . . if one had been there to see it.

Arthur—who had entered the room just in time to catch the entire tableau—*had* seen it. But Jennifer did not see *him*, neither then nor when she took the boy across the room to find another book—his hand held trustingly in hers.

Withdrawing quietly from the scene, Arthur returned to his office, asked his secretary to handle all his calls and inquiries, and shut the door. He walked over to the window and looked unseeingly out on the iron-gray bay.

* * *

The next time, she came on a rainy afternoon. Evidently a lot of other people agreed with her that a bookstore was the best place to be on such a day. Long lines piled up behind the cash registers, and many people waited with questions. The clerks, she noticed, tried to be helpful and answered all questions politely and with the obvious willingness to go the second mile. They knew many customers by name.

Even the Spanish girl. From time to time, Jennifer saw the girl turn to see if a certain gentleman remained in his office. Then, when Mr. Bond finally *did* come out, the girl's cheeks flamed as she looked everywhere but in his direction. A number of people clustered around him, asking questions, and each one received that same warm smile and attitude of eager helpfulness.

Then the Spanish girl went up to her boss to ask a question. Jennifer didn't fail to notice both the smile he gave his lovely clerk and the rapt expression in the girl's eyes. *Hmm.*

She moved on to the American writers section, looking for some of her favorite authors. *Oh! what a selection of Harold Bell Wright! I've never seen this many in one place before!* She took down a dust jacketed *Exit.* No sooner had she done so than she felt a presence behind her.

"Are you into Wright?" a familiar voice asked.

She turned, smiled (*I like her dimples,* Arthur observed to himself), and said, "Well, sort of. I've read five or six, but I've never seen this one—or, for that matter, a number of the others here. Rarely do I see more than a few of his books in any one place."

"Well, there's a reason for that . . . uh . . . Miss—it *is* Miss . . . ?"

"Yes," and she found his steady gaze, kindly though it was, more than a bit disconcerting. "My last name is O'Riley."

"Mine," he grinned a little wickedly, "is Bond. But not" (obviously he had used this line many times before) "James . . . but Arthur."

"And I answer to Jennifer," she said, blushing.

Ignoring the opening, he returned to Wright, "Well, Miss O'Riley, Wright books are hard to get and harder to keep in stock. Might I ask which ones you've read?"

"Well, the first of his books I read when I was only seventeen. Read it one beautiful day on California's Feather River Canyon. I was visiting a favorite aunt and uncle at the time. I'll never forget it; it changed my life."

"I'd guess it was one of his Social Gospel trilogy," he broke in.

"Trilogy?" she asked. "There's a trilogy? The one I read was *The Calling of Dan Matthews,* and it really changed my life."

"Oh?" he asked quizzically.

She stumbled a bit for words, finally stammering out, "I just don't know how to go on . . . and I don't know yet if . . . if . . . uh . . ."

"If I am a Christian?" he finished for her.

"Yes."

"Well, I am. . . . Why do you ask?"

"Oh . . . it's just that *The Calling of Dan Matthews* gave me a new vision of God, of His all-inclusiveness. I'm afraid I had been rather elitist before I read that book."

He laughed (conspiratorially, she thought). "I agree, Miss O'Riley; it hit me that way, too. Only, I had read *That Printer of Udels* first (by the way, it anchors the trilogy), so I was somewhat prepared for his contention that Christ's entire earthly ministry was not about doctrine at all . . . but about . . ."

". . . service," she broke in softly.

"Yes, service for others," he agreed.

They talked a long time about Wright that day, and after that about other authors of mutual interest as well. Some, they loved in common; others they did their best to convert the other to.

He had always felt he could more than hold his own in any battle of wits, but he discovered that in Jennifer, he had met his match. One day, as they sparred back and forth on the historical romances of Rafael Sabatini (while each had favorites, both agreed on the one that stood out above all others, *Scaramouche,* that great tale of the French Revolution), he grimaced—*she never misses a trick . . . not a nuance escapes her!*

Not long after, during another visit, she found a copy of a book she'd searched for . . . for years: Gene Stratton Porter's *The Fire Bird.* She quickly found a quiet niche, settled down in an easy chair, turned up the lamp, and began leafing through the book. She held no illusions about buying it, though. Beautiful and rare, true—but the price was far too high for *her* budget.

Then she heard voices, one of which sounded very familiar. She pulled in her feet so as to be as inconspicuous as possible. When the voices drew nearer, she drew her legs under her, yoga style. Since the speakers sat down in the alcove just before hers, she couldn't help but overhear. "I just don't know what I'm going to do, Mr. Bond!" quivered a woman's voice: "I really don't. Lately . . . I . . . I . . . just feel even the good Lord has forsaken me."

"*That,* Mrs. Henry, I can assure you is not true. The Lord *never* forsakes His children," he responded.

"Oh, but Mr. Bond, you just don't *know!* Or you wouldn't be so sure. My oldest son—you remember Chris! . . . Well, he's on drugs. Worse than that, he's become a pusher. . . ." Her voice broke. "And Dana. I . . . I . . . I just found out she's pregnant. I just can't believe it. She grew up so faithful at attending church every week. And the man, the man who . . . uh . . . uh . . ."

"The father of the unborn baby?"

"Yes . . . he attends our church, too."

"Oh? . . . Are they planning to marry?"

"That's the worst part. He says it's all her fault for not taking precautions. Won't have anything more to do with her. And Dana's near desperate. I'm afraid she'll, she'll . . ." And again her voice broke.

The other voice broke in, firmly and kindly: "Mrs. Henry, there is no time to lose. Is Dana home this afternoon?"

Answered in the affirmative, he led her out, and, after explaining to the clerks that an emergency had come up, he and Mrs. Henry hurried through the heavy rain to their cars.

For a long time Jennifer just sat there, thinking. *Just what kind of bookstore— what kind of man—is this?*

She came back within the week . . . and shamelessly stayed within listening range of where he worked. She simply *had* to know, for sure, what manner of man this was. So many times before, she'd been disappointed, disillusioned—so why should this one prove to be any different?

She was, by turns, amazed, then moved, by what she overheard. Apparently, he possessed endless patience, for she never heard him lose his temper, no matter what the provocation. Even with bores, who insisted on talking on and on about themselves. She discovered that while most of his customers asked book-related questions, a surprisingly large number felt overwhelmed by life and its problems. In Arthur, they found . . . perhaps not always solutions, but at least a listening, sympathetic ear. In used bookstores, she had discovered, there appears to be an implied assumption: one finds an ear, no matter how stupid, inane, or ridiculous the topic may be. In that respect, used bookstores function as courts of last resort, the last chance to be heard before outright despair sets in. But, in Arthur's case, it went far beyond mere listening—for he genuinely *cared!*

* * *

At last came August, and with it pre-session. Vacation was over, for school would begin in a few weeks. So busy was she that it was almost Labor Day before she got back to Pandora's Books. Just as she was leaving, he came out of his office and smiled at her. On the confidence of that smile, she walked over to him and asked if he could spare a moment.

"Of *course!*" he replied, steering her into a quieter room and seating her by an open window, for the heat had *finally* broken, and the cool bay breeze felt like heaven.

During the small talk that followed, she became increasingly aware of how strongly this man affected her, his tangible synthesis of strength, wisdom, and kindness. She was more aware of being near him than she had ever been with any other man. Stumbling a bit over her words, she asked him if he ever spoke to students about books, not just singly but in the schoolroom itself.

"Often, Miss O'Riley."

For some unaccountable reason, she blushed.

Pandora chose this moment to demand attention, and he lifted her up into his arms, where she ecstatically began to purr and knead her claws into him.

"You see, Miss O'Riley," he continued, "they represent our future. There can be no higher priority than children."

She found herself inviting him to speak to her class, and he gladly accepted.

As she drove home and her Camaro left a trail of greenish-yellow leaves dancing in her wake, she acknowledged to herself that she'd just, by that act, set forces in motion—forces that might breach almost any wall she'd built up through the years.

Apprehensive she was, a little. But she sang an old love song over and over all the way home, not realizing, until her garage door opened on command, just what she'd been singing.

* * *

He *came!* And the children loved him! He came with a big box of books and sat down on the floor with them, holding them enthralled by the stories that came from those books . . . and the men and women who illustrated them. And he answered each of the many questions they asked; the ones he couldn't, he promised to answer the day their teacher brought them on a field trip to his wildlife sanctuary/bookstore, when they could meet Pandora. Jennifer pulled back from her usual focal center to give him the opportunity to be in control. She needn't have bothered; she knew now that when he walked into a room, it was as if he were iridescent, for he attracted all eyes just as if he shone like the sun. Just as was true—though she didn't know it—of herself.

She watched his every move, listened to his every word, and watched the quicksilver moods as they cavorted on his face and danced in his blue-gray eyes—

eyes with the impishness of the eternal child in them. Like the legendary Pied Piper of Hamelin, he so enthralled that the children would have followed him *anywhere.*

And he, though apparently he saw nothing but the children, never missed a nuance of her. The vision she made, leaning against the window, would hang in the galleries of his mind for all time—a Dante Gabriel Rossetti dream woman. Her long bronze hair, ignited by the late morning sun, her emerald green dress, and her seize-the-day face added up to far more than mere beauty.

Before he left, he let each child choose a favorite book—and left the rest for the room library. Then, after reminding them to "come see Pandora soon," he was gone . . . and the halcyon day clouded over. But the sun came back out again when one curious little boy sneaked to the window and caught sight of Mr. Bond getting into his '57 Thunderbird. His awestruck "Wow!" brought the entire class to the window in seconds, and they all waved—and he, catching the motion at the window, waved back as the coral sand convertible sped out of sight.

But not out of memory.

But just to make sure, that afternoon a florist delivered a large autumn floral display, crowned by a couple of book-topped spears, and at the very top, a goldish-brown cat.

That night, he called: Did she want to go with him to the Kennedy Center to hear the Vienna Choir Boys? . . . *Was the Pope Catholic?*

Not long after, his second call came, asking her to attend church service with him. After that, the telephone worked both ways. Concerts, the many galleries and exhibits of the Smithsonian, opera, rides to the seashore, to quaint restaurants in old inns, and hikes along mountain trails—all this brought roses to her cheeks and a glow into her eyes.

After Thanksgiving dinner at her folks', he told her to bundle up for a rather chilly ride. Always, it seemed with him, the top stayed firmly down—he reveled in the 360-degree view. On and on the Bird sped, and as she nestled down, the excitement brimming over in her eyes and the way her sapphire blue paisley scarf set off her flaming mane of hair—well, it made it mighty difficult to keep his eyes on the road.

The population thinned out as the Bird's deep throat rumbled into old St. Mary's City.

Here, they stopped by the river for a while, ostensibly to watch the geese, but in reality, because he felt reflective.

"You know, Jennifer, I think it's time I told you a little more about my failed marriage."

"That's up to you, Arthur."

"Let's see, how do I start? . . . Well, I had known Marilyn for a number of years; we attended the same parochial high school, same college—even the same church. My folks were good friends with her folks—had been for many years. We liked the same things, shared many of the same dreams."

She listened, gazing out at the river.

"Actually," Arthur laughed, a strangely undefinable laugh, "I don't think I ever actually proposed—we just drifted into it. All our friends, our families, our folks, took it for granted. . . . So we married. We loved each other. *That,* I'm sure of. It was to be for life—at least it was for me."

There was a long pause, as he searched for the right words.

"We were married about eighteen months. Then, one never-to-be-forgotten spring morning, after breakfast, she announced that marriage was 'a bore,' 'a drag,' and that she wanted to regain her freedom."

A pause. Then in a flat voice, he continued: "So she divorced me, and found another—several others, actually. . . . That was about twelve years ago, but it seems like yesterday. . . . Oh, I foundered for a time; my self-esteem was at its all-time low."

Then he brightened: "But God saw me through. I escaped to the New England coast and stayed there a long time—healing. It was there that the epiphany came to me: Pandora's Books."

"Oh!" she breathed, half a sigh, half a paean.

"Yes, a dream bookstore—unlike any I had ever seen or heard about. But the Lord showed me that mere business success would not be enough: I must also care for His sheep. *That* would be my ministry. And the frosting on the cake . . ."

". . . was Pandora," she finished.

"Yes, Pandora." He smiled, started the engine, and they were again out on the highway, heading south.

I'm so glad he told me! she murmured to herself as the car gathered speed. *He didn't walk out on her! That's what I was afraid of. . . . He had to have been hurt more than I was, yet he didn't let it destroy him. There was closure—a long time ago. . . .* And joyously, *There's a clear road ahead! Oh Lord, thank You!* And her heart began to sing.

Then she lost all track of time as the Bird raced down the peninsula, churning up waves of gold, brown, orange, crimson, and green leaves in their wake. Suddenly, only a narrow, gray strip of land lay ahead, banked by white-capped blue below and white-winged gulls in blue sky above. The Bird nosed into a parking space at the end of the road—Route 5, dead end. Since it was both cold and blustery, they had it all to themselves.

For a few minutes they just sat there, watching and listening to the gulls. She wondered what he was thinking.

Leaning back, his hands behind his head, he finally broke into her reverie: "You know, Jennifer, this is what I miss most. Solitude. The solitude you can still find out west and up north. So many people live here that, after a while, one gets claustrophobic. At least I do. If anything ever moves me away from this bay, it will be that. Well, that and my beloved mountains. I miss them."

Suddenly, he shifted in his seat and laughed. "Am I ever the gabby one today! Enough about me. What about *you?* What is *your* story? Hasn't some steel-clad knight tried to gallop away with you?"

Shyly, she answered, "Y-e-e-s."

"Well, what happened?" he demanded, an impish look in his eyes. "Fess up: I did my stint, now it's *your* turn."

So she told him . . . and took a while doing it. When she finally finished, he sat in silence a while, then smiled. "I'm glad. Someday I may tell you why."

"Someday you may, huh," she laughed, her eyes narrowing.

"You know, Jennifer, your voice has bells in it . . . your laugh, most of all. Even on the phone, I hear bells ringing when you speak. You radiate happiness."

She blushed, started to say something, then stopped.

"Go on," he chuckled. "Might as well get it out."

"Oh!" she said, trying to slow her racing heart. "It's just that I've been happy a lot lately . . . and . . . and," refusing to meet his eyes, *"you're* to blame."

There! It was out, and her eyes fell, unable to meet his.

Silence thundered in her ears, and when at last she looked up, he was looking out to sea with an enigmatic look on his face. His body had tensed, his face was now rigid. . . . She felt utterly humiliated by her admission.

Then he turned, placed his hand on hers butterfly-briefly, and said, "Well, it's getting late. What do you say to heading back?"

All the way back, she wallowed in misery: *Why did I wreck what had been so perfect? Why change gears when I was just beginning to gain momentum in the lower one?*

Once she caught him eyeing her pensively.

When he walked her to her door, they didn't banter as usual. He didn't ask her for another date, just—in a flat tone of voice—"Thank you, Jennifer, for a perfect Thanksgiving!"

* * *

That was a long *long* night for Jennifer. To herself, she wailed, *Stupid me! I've blown it! I took a wonderful friendship, just beginning to bud, and wrecked it. Might just as well have demanded the full-blown rose! . . . But that's just it: I'm in love with him. Been in love with him for a long time—just refused to admit it. He storms me in his quiet, gentle way. I . . . I . . . I've never met anyone before who lights up every room he's in—at least for me. I know it's shameless: but here I am—in my thirties—having never known passion (wondering if I even had it in me!), and now, with this man, I yearn for him, long for him, desire him, with every inch of my body, heart, and soul!*

Her thoughts raced on. *Friendship alone is no longer enough even if, all too obviously, it is to him. My passionate heart cries for far more. I cannot be merely another in a long line of friendships—perhaps even romances—with him.*

If only, if only, though, I had waited, perhaps it would have come.

Oh why, oh Lord, did I do it! . . . . Oh, God . . . to find my soul's other half—after all these long years—and then to lose him because of my big big mouth!

And she wept through that endless night.

When he called, as usual, to ask her to attend church with him, she turned him down in an icy voice, then cut the conversation short by saying, "I'm sorry . . . but I've gotta run; I'm late!" and hung up. Then she *was* miserable, for in reality she had nothing else to do at all, and an entire evening to mope about it.

* * *

Jennifer loved the Christmas season, a time when being a child again became an accepted thing. With what joy she always greeted the wreaths and garlands, the multicolored lights on the neighborhood eaves and trees, the Advent candles, the Christmas trees seen through the windows, the Christmas carols played continuously by radio stations. This year, though, she just wished it would go away. Even in her schoolroom. True, she decorated it in the usual way, drilled the children for the big Christmas program, and helped them make personalized gifts for those dearest to them. But it all seemed hollow, all a sham. Even God, she felt, irrationally, had somehow let her down: *Lord, how could You do this to me? How could You let me make such a fool of myself!*

She no longer kidded herself about what Arthur meant to her. Or that he might be but a passing fancy that would go away. No, for better or for worse, he'd be a deep-rooted part of her as long as she lived.

He did not call again. Several times—nay, a hundred times!—she felt the urge to call him and apologize for her curtness on the phone, but her lacerated pride just would not let her.

Her last papers corrected, scores added up, gifts accepted from each of her students, and the big program—to which she'd once planned to invite Arthur—going off without a hitch . . . yet none of it meant anything to her. Nothing at all.

On that dismal winter evening, she just sat there in her not-even-decorated-this-year townhouse, wallowing in misery and self-pity, wishing for him—yearning for him—and dreading Christmas week.

The phone rang.

She answered it, but no bells rang in her voice, just a subdued "hello!" Almost, she hung up when she heard his voice on the other end, inwardly raging because his voice still possessed this power over her, giving her goose bumps. . . . It just didn't seem fair! But there was something different in his voice, almost a pleading note. He had a big favor to ask of her, he said.

"A favor?" she snapped, and then could have choked her misbehaving other self for that snippiness.

Silence swirled around her. Then he continued, more haltingly this time. He had a big favor to ask, yes, but with a qualifier or two thrown in. First of all, he wanted her to share the *Messiah* with him at Washington's National Cathedral, and secondly, he wanted to show her something of extreme importance.

When the silence on the other end of the line continued, he gulped and added, "If you'll accept just this once, I'll promise not to ever bother you again."

Seeing no graceful way out of it, she grudgingly parted with an undernourished "yes."

There! Finished! That would end it. No ellipsis, no dash, no period. Period! Period! Period! . . . But three periods would be an open-ended ellipsis! shouted an irrational thought from a far corner of her brain.

Her mind raced, her thoughts milled in chaotic confusion: *I shouldn't have said yes—that I'd go. But I'd hate to miss out on going! . . . I don't think I can handle being close to him again—I'm so sure my face will give me away if my big mouth doesn't. . . . Yet, how can I possibly give up this one last time (the last time we'll ever be together)? . . . . Oh, it will tear my heart out to be close to him and not be able to touch him! Not to be able . . . Oh! Oh! Yet I don't want him to take anyone else there! Certainly—make that double certainly!—not that Spanish beauty! Oh! What am I going to wear?*

The big evening (the *last* evening! she promised herself) finally came.

She dressed carefully in her favorite blue gown, a Diane Fries she had purchased at Nordstrom in a rare fit of recklessness. She'd make it a swan song to remember. Then she put on her heavy black cashmere coat, bought on sale just before I Magnin closed.

The doorbell rang, her pulse quickened. She forced herself to walk very slowly to the door, lest she appear too eager. *Oh, I'm a despicable vixen!* she reprimanded her misbehaving other self.

When she opened it and saw him standing there, in spite of her well-planned intentions, sapphire stars sparkled in her eyes, and her cheeks crimsoned. For he was so . . . so . . . . so detestably dear.

At the curb, its motor purring, was a car she'd not seen before, a Mercedes 560, in color a suspiciously emerald sort of green.

"Wouldn't dare park the Bird in D.C." was his only explanation.

Outside the window, the white of the year's first snowfall enveloped the world. Christmas CDs played softly through the sophisticated sound system, and she relaxed a little in spite of herself.

Neither said much during the ride to the cathedral.

They had a tough time finding a parking space, but finally joined the well-dressed throng filling the streets. Excitement flooded her cheeks, and once or twice she trembled as his hand brushed hers.

Inside the world's sixth largest cathedral, all was Christmas, and he moved, with her just behind him, toward the nave. He took her hand now to keep her close. Eventually they arrived at the spot where he felt the acoustics to be nearly perfect and found a pillar on which to lean, for the seats were all taken.

Then the organ found its voice, shaking the near-century-in-the-making building, and chills went up her spine. Pipe organs had that power over her. She sneaked a sideways glance at him and felt satisfied by the look of awe on his face. Then the orchestra, then the soloists, then the choirs, and then she lost all track of time as Handel transported her through the drama of the ages.

Through it all, she remained aware of him, but in a sort of haze. He left once and brought back two chairs; she sank down with a sigh of relief. After a couple of hours, unconsciously declaring a temporary truce, she took advantage of his tall frame next to her and leaned her head against him. She felt him tremble when a draft of cold air blew a strand of her flame-colored hair across his face.

Soaring upward, her soul drank deeply of the majesty of the mighty columns and graceful arches that portrayed the architectural yearning for the Eternal.

The words and music and organ and choirs and soloists and cathedral battered her sensibilities into a pulp. It was too much of a sensory overload for mere flesh and blood. During the "Hallelujah Chorus," when she stood at his side, she again felt him tremble and peeped sideways to find him wiping away tears. Since she was crying too, she felt a renewed sense of kinship with him.

The crowd was unbelievably quiet as they found their way out, almost as if words seemed far too fragile to accommodate such divine freight.

On the slippery road again, neither spoke, and the sound system remained silent, as if anything else right now would be anticlimactic. For this she inwardly thanked him, for his sensitivity and empathy. For not shattering the mood.

So surreal was it all that she didn't even notice they had passed her highway exit until the Mercedes veered off Highway 50 onto Riva Road. To her raised eyebrows, he merely smiled and said, "Remember, there's more yet to this promised evening."

As the traffic thinned out south of Annapolis, and the flocked evergreens flashed by, he began to speak, slowly, haltingly.

"Undoubtedly . . . you . . . you . . . uh, wondered about my strange response to your . . . uh . . . to what you said about yourself the last time we were together."

She stiffened. *How dare he bring up that utterly humiliating afternoon when he rejected my stupid disclosure of my inner feelings. How dare he!*

But he plowed on, not looking at her. "You see, Jen,"—he'd never called her by her family pet name before!—"I was so wounded, so scarred, by the rejection I told you about . . . that I determined that never again," and here he struggled for control, then continued, "never again would I let a woman get that close to me."

He paused, and she hardly dared breathe.

"But it's been hard, Jen, because I'm still young . . . and lonely. It's been very hard."

Inadvertently, her lesser self got in another lick: "The beautiful black-haired girl who works for you?"

He almost hit a tree, but when he turned toward her, his face had relaxed just a little: "How did you know?"

"I have eyes. Any woman could have told you."

There was a long silence as he searched for the right words. Finally, as if he had given up finding any better ones, the refrain again: "It's been hard." But he did not tell her that it was the Spanish beauty's lack of tenderness, her repulsing of the little crying boy, that had turned the tide of his life.

Neither did he tell her about the effect *she* had made on him that same day—a Raphael Madonna, tenderly holding a child.

After a time, he continued. "You see, Jen, I couldn't take such rejection twice in one lifetime. I'm afraid it would . . . uh . . . destroy me!" He paused again. "Marriage for me is for life—even if our society seems to disagree with me." Here, his words seemed sadly bitter to the wondering woman at his side. "And marriage, without God to cement it, is dead end! I don't see how any marriage can last a lifetime without a Higher Power to anchor in. All around me, I see marriage after marriage, live-in relationships galore, collapse, so few making it through. I have been afraid. I'm not ashamed to admit it, Jen; I've been terribly afraid to even consider marriage again!"

She remained silent. Numb.

"As for children and what divorce or separation does to them . . . there are simply no words in the dictionary terrible enough to fully describe what it does to them, to their feelings of self-worth. I see it every day. And I don't yet know what to do, what to say, to their anguish—anguish so intense it's long since wrung out all the tears they can cry."

And she, remembering those lonely, deep-scarred wounded ones in her classes, could only nod her head.

"And then *you* came," he added, groping for the right words. "You scared me."

He caught her whispered *"Scared?"*

"Yes. . . . Scared. For you were, well, what I never had, yet had always wanted. In a way, too good to be true. Jen, I never expected to find such a woman as you. So when you told me—last Thanksgiving—that I . . . that I made you happy, like an absolute fool, I panicked! I had blocked such a future out of the realm of the possible for so many years that when it came, I just, just didn't know how . . ."

Suddenly, he slowed and turned down a familiar road, now a fairyland in snow. Her heart began to thud, thud, thud, so loudly that she felt certain he must overhear it.

Then he turned down a road she had never noticed before, and made a long wide turn. Then, directly ahead, in a blaze of holiday lights, there stood Pandora's Books. It was so beautiful, her lips O'd, and her hands flew to her face. She didn't see his relieved smile.

Inside, festive music played in every room, only all the same track this time. Christmas decorations were everywhere, as were lights and trees of various sizes. "I've always loved Christmas; never really grew up, I guess," he said simply. Unknowingly, she groped for his hand.

He showed her each room, and her delighted response and the restored bells in her voice were all he could have hoped for. Finally they came back to the office area, and he stepped briefly behind the counter where he must have flicked a switch, for suddenly silence shattered the mood, and she was alone with him in the big building.

He walked back to her, and she raised her emerald eyes to his, seeking to find something that had not been there before. Suddenly she heard music again, froze for a moment, and whispered, *"Étude in E."*

"Yes."

"Why, Arthur? I don't understand what you're trying to . . ."

Softly placing his finger on her lips, he whispered, "Listen!"

She listened. And, as she knew it would—it always had—it melted her. And, as she knew she would—she always had—she cried.

Fire blazed through her tears, and she accused, "How could you! You know how that affects me—I saw you watching me that day."

Know? Yes, he knew. She was right. *It's all come down to this question, this moment,* he thought. *I hurt her terribly by my inexcusable fear of commitment. . . . And now I must answer. But one thing is certain: This is no time for half-hearted measures. . . . Words, words can be such inadequate things! How can I make her know?*

Gathering her in his arms, he answered softly, "I just *had* to, dear . . . dearest."

Her wounded pride struggled to assert itself. *How dare he assume I'd forgive him this easily for what he has put me through? How* dare *he!*

In the end, her pride lost. Gentle, he remained, but as immovable as Gibraltar. The *Étude* was on his side too—it was two against one. She felt her resistance ebbing. Then she made the mistake of trying to read the expression on his face—not easy, considering the dim light in the room. . . . But what she saw there closed forever all avenues of escape. It was love. Love undiluted, unqualified, undistilled, unreserved, undivided. He had cleared the deck of his heart of everything else but *her.*

Her struggles ceased, and all the lights of the world came on in her eyes as her arms stole up and closed behind his neck. Then it was, as the shackles of fear and regret fell clanging to the floor, that he started to tell her in mere words how much he loved her, but she, cutting his words off with her lips, showed him a better way. . . . A far better way.

* * *

Some time later, he sensed a familiar presence at his ankles. Looking down, but not releasing her from the prison of his arms by so much as one link, he smiled: "Sorry Pandora, you jealous thing. From now on . . . you're gonna have to *share!*"

AFTERWORD

Unbeknownst to me, I've been preparing to write this story all my life. Each of the thousands of used bookstores I've known—many that I've loved— represent the gestation period. Also part of the mix is Annapolis's Haunted Bookstore, with Mike, the big tabby cat who undisputedly ruled its premises. Occasionally, he could even be found sleeping in the street-side display window! Sadly, due to the escalating of the rent, Mike and that wonderful bookstore no longer grace Maryland's capital city. And there is some of Christopher Morley's moving book, *The Haunted Bookshop* stirred in, as well. Actually, the story represents a synthesis of my own dream bookstore, had I only the money and time to make it happen.

Étude in E has been called by many "the most beautiful étude ever composed." Chopin dedicated it to his dear friend, Franz Liszt, and it remained Chopin's personal favorite of all his own études. Norman Luboff recorded it, in perhaps as romantic a recording as has ever been made, in his Norman Luboff Choir *Reverie.*

The deeply wounded Jennifer and Arthur—each of us knows them personally for they represent a far too large part of our "love 'em, leave 'em, and never count the cost" society. As for Pandora, in real life she *was* Pandora, the pampered Himalayan who ruled our book-laden house for over thirteen years. Life without that furry presence, that constant companion, that flopper-against-me every time I sit or lie down or try to write something worth reading, hurts every time I remember. But always, in this story, she will live on.

* * * * *